The Good Wife
and Philosophy

Popular Culture and Philosophy® Series Editor: George A. Reisch

For full details of all Popular Culture and Philosophy® books, visit www.opencourtbooks.com.

Popular Culture and Philosophy®

The Good Wife and Philosophy

Temptations of Saint Alicia

Edited by

KIMBERLY BALTZER-JARAY

and

ROBERT ARP

OPEN COURT
Chicago

Volume 76 in the series, Popular Culture and Philosophy ®, edited by George A. Reisch

To order books from Open Court, call toll-free 1-800-815-2280, or visit our website at www.opencourtbooks.com.

Open Court Publishing Company is a division of Carus Publishing Company, dba ePals Media.

Printed and bound in the United States of America.

ISBN: 978-0-8126-9824-4 (trade paperback)

Library of Congress Control Number: 2013939106

We were deeply saddened in August 2012 to hear of the death of Tony Scott, legendary filmmaker, one of The Good Wife*'s executive producers, and brother of Ridley Scott. Scott Free Productions, formed by the Scott brothers, produced and helped finance the show. We owe Tony a debt of gratitude for* The Good Wife*. This volume is dedicated to him and his incredible legacy as a great movie artist. Cheers, Tony.*

Contents

The Good Wife and the Real Life

KIMBERLY BALTZER-JARAY AND ROBERT ARP

"The first thing we do, let's kill all the lawyers."

In Shakespeare's *King Henry VI Part 2*, there's a famous dialogue that occurs amongst the rebels led by Jack Cade, who after a successful revolt begins to discuss his plans for his ideal kingdom: free beer, free food, equality amongst people, and no money. To which the ever-mocking Dick the Butcher responds, "The first thing we do, let's kill all the lawyers."

This was a scene of comic relief, and many a laugh has been had at it, but what makes it effective is its irony: first, we're listening to men who are murderers, thieves, and rapists discussing a utopian, libertarian kind of society, and second, one of the worst amongst them sees lawyers as the villains, the scourge of society. Lawyers take parchment, the skin of innocent lambs, and scribble a man's fate; some men rob you with a sword or gun or a swift hand, and others with a fountain pen and a law book.

However, this is a very one-sided view of lawyers, a narrow profile offered by criminals who only see the courtroom and the jailhouse, and never what happens behind the scenes in the office or at home: the efforts, the sweat, the tears . . . the human side to being a lawyer. Lawyers—whether you want to admit it or not—are people too.

The groundbreaking, long-running TV show *Law and Order* offers us a small glimpse of lawyers outside of court, but remains focused on things related to work; we see lawyers at their office, at the police station, and at the houses of key witnesses. But we don't see executive ADA Jack McCoy at home in his PJs eating mac and cheese with a glass of scotch, nor do we see any of his assistant ADAs pregnant or at home tending to children and spouses. At one point, Nora Lewin replaces Adam Schiff as the DA of New York County and McCoy's boss—we had a female DA who had been a reputable law professor! That lasted about forty-eight episodes, then Arthur Branch arrived, but you never saw her outside the office setting in her sweats and scruffies. You knew nothing of her life beyond the desk. But, then again, many of the other pre–*Good Wife* law shows were that way—lawyers at work and play, but not at home being real people.

The Good Wife has changed this. It has provided a glimpse of this other side of the story through several central characters, men and women alike. We see their romantic problems, interoffice dramas with colleagues, issues of personal identity and privacy, and their struggles to find a balance between family obligations and work demands—all this is in addition to the immense and ongoing creative strategies for applying the law and its precedents they must come up with to win cases. We witness the interactions between lawyers and clients inside and outside the courtroom, the times when the two bond closely and work well together, and the times when there is great friction and discord. We experience the moments when the law is skillfully manipulated, sometimes justly and other times unjustly, and we see the consequences of such actions.

Most important, the main character is a woman, and we see her struggles and triumphs inside and outside the law office. Alicia is an educated, middle-aged woman attempting to juggle raising teenagers, a hectic job, a marriage rocked by a cheating scandal, an annoying mother-in-law, a boss she has feelings for, a firm that is struggling to get out of bankruptcy, and a host of other madness that can be seen as not out of the ordinary. Best of all, she isn't one hundred percent perfect in the way she handles it all. In fact, she barely keeps her head above water at times and some of her decisions are not always the perceived 'right' ones. Now this is a woman many of us can relate to!

Her marriage to Peter is a great example: Alicia has kept it intact on paper but in every other way they have been separated (except legally, they didn't have paperwork). She kept it this way even when engaging in a romantic relationship with Will Gardner, her boss and her college "love that got away" sweetheart. She even kept up appearances of being Peter's "good wife" during the political campaign, just for the sake of potential victory. This was a controversial choice; some people were applauding her for 'cheating' on Peter, some were upset that she didn't just dump Peter, get it over with if she couldn't trust him, and move on with Will, and others were concerned she was just rebounding with her boss and that was highly inappropriate, cheating or not.

Was she selfish? Was she cowardly? Was she being vengeful? Was she stupid? Or was she simply being true to herself and doing what she thought best for her life situation? The thing is, there is no right answer here—every decision has good and bad elements—and that's life. *The Good Wife* is a show that at least attempts to portray life in all its mess and grey areas. It doesn't just regurgitate the current morally or socially acceptable choice and lifestyle.

As the episodes progress, we see Alicia growing as a woman, a mother, and a lawyer. This growth happens as she sheds false and unrealistic expectations of what a mother or a wife should be, as she realizes that her own wants should be important and valued, and as she carves out her unique niche at the firm and in the practice of law itself. Alicia, like so many middle-aged professional women, is rediscovering who she is and questioning the things she once accepted as true. As she does this, we do it too, and many preconceived social norms about women get challenged. At times, the same can be said about our preconceived notions of lawyers. Sometimes, not all the time.

In presenting this side of being a lawyer, and a *female* lawyer, all kinds of philosophical areas of investigation appear: ethics, theories of justice, feminism, privacy rights, epistemology, social and political philosophy, and others. Our authors illuminate the various philosophical threads sewn into every episode of *The Good Wife* and the characters and situations that make up the mosaic quilt of the show, revealing the complexities of being a lawyer and the world of law that lawyers must work within. *The Good Wife* is so much more than just brilliant, pathbreaking TV—it opens portals into philosophy.

So, rather than kill them all right away, let's philosophically analyze them first and see where that takes us. If that doesn't work, then we sharpen our blades.

I

Ethically Speaking

1
Legal Ethics! Really?

JUDITH ANDRE

*T*he *Good Wife* is filled with ethical tension. Should Alicia stay with Peter? Help him win parole? Should she sleep with Will? Is using Peter's contacts to help her firm ethical ("Unplugged")? Should she use Peter's insider knowledge to win a case ("Conjugal")?

Ethical issues basic to the practice of law emerge throughout the series. These issues are faced by every lawyer, not just the firm of Lockhart Gardner. Sometimes the issues are obvious. Judges, for instance, have convictions and biases of the liberal-or-conservative kind, and personal ones as well: Peter was well known in the courts where Alicia practices, and some judges, well, *prejudge* her (pun intended). It's hard to know whether their decisions are in fact biased, but it's obvious that bias is wrong, especially in the legal realm where "justice is blind" and judges are supposed to remain objective and neutral.

Other legal ethical issues are more complicated. In Season One's "Conjugal" Alicia spends a (sexless) night with Peter in prison to get information she needs to win a case. The script suggests this is a professional gray area—uncomfortably like insider trading. In another episode, Will asks Alicia to snatch evidence from their client's apartment before the police can get there. "You're *well* within the law," he says. He backs down a bit after she gives him a skeptical look:

"Well, you're *within* the law." She does what he asks, however—she gets the goods ("Hi"), another move that is both legally and ethically questionable.

Kalinda, an enigmatic and often dark character, uses tactics that can be downright illegal—in addition to being unethical—yet the firm uses what she finds. "This evidence isn't admissible in court, but it's useful *outside* of court," she claims in the Season Two episode "Heart." The evidence can be used to pressure the opposition with a threat of exposing their client's "heartless" insurance practices. In that episode, because we feel so strongly for the pregnant woman whose insurance company refuses to pay for what she needs, we're glad for the underhanded tactic despite the fact that we know that what Kalinda is doing is ethically questionable. Still, Will's date in the Season Two episode "Cleaning House" speaks for many of us: "I don't get lawyers. They always seem to be out to trick people."

The Good Wife is a Hollywood show that mostly doesn't represent reality—it's escapism, and when we stop to think about its fictional situations, we have to "willingly suspend our disbelief." In Season Three's "Long Way Home," for instance, Alicia discovers her client has perjured himself. Will tells her she can use the testimony, since she hadn't known he was going to lie, let alone encouraged him to do it. But Will is wrong: knowingly using perjured testimony is a clear violation of professional lawyerly standards. Disciplinary Rule 7-102(A)(1)—which was adopted by the American Bar Association in 1970—states: "a lawyer shall not knowingly use perjured testimony or false evidence."

However, the show does point out something that is part of reality: legal victories are often won outside of courtroom litigation. What are American courts really for? Can legal tactics that have become standard bring about "liberty and justice for all"? Do the ethically questionable moves that lawyers make on *The Good Wife* and in reality serve the cause of justice, or subvert it? Is lawyerly work underhanded trickery?

Zealous Advocacy

It seems so, at times. Consider this example. In the Season One episode "Unorthodox," Alicia discovers that the firm has supported a client by simply exhausting the other side's funds. Delaying tactics keep the case from getting to court and run up the tab until the plaintiff can't afford to continue. Alicia is shocked, but Will is unruffled; this is standard procedure when the opponent has "shallow pockets."

Will's right; this strategy is standard, and in full accord with codes of legal ethics. Here the interesting questions begin. If the point of our legal system is to serve justice, and such tactics don't do that, why are they accepted? In fact, bankrupting your opponent quite explicitly interferes with the pursuit of justice: If a case never goes before a judge, no weighing of evidence will happen, no verdict will be rendered. The party with the most money will win—a rather familiar idea, but not an attractive one.

Lawyers call such maneuvers *zealous advocacy* on behalf of the client, and endorse them as part of a two-level commitment. Ultimately, lawyers are devoted to the rule of law. It's what makes the country work, what makes it possible for strangers with competing interests to work together. The law provides an orderly way of resolving disputes that, in contrast to private vengeance, doesn't usually escalate into vigilante mobs or deteriorate into endless feuds. The legal system does this by providing a set of impersonal procedures whose results will be enforced by the power of the state. Alicia, Diane, and Will obviously value the law and are proud to be part of it.

So, once again, why do they interfere with its working? Delaying tactics can prevent a case from ever being adjudicated. Removing evidence makes the police less likely to find the truth. Lockhart Gardner does these things because lawyers serve the law by serving their clients. Lawyers view zealous advocacy as their most sacred commitment; but can it be taken too far? In the Season One episode "Running," reacting to the fact that she knows her client is a murderer,

Alicia asks Will, "At what point is doing our job . . . wrong?" And he responds, "When it fails our client." In an earlier episode titled "Boom" from the same season, Will uses racial profiling to defend a client who has been the victim of the same strategy. Will's defense: "We're going to step nicely past the ironies here and defend our client." The obligation of zealous advocacy is omnipresent in the series, usually implicit but sometimes explicit.

Some Good Competition

Much less explicit in the show—and in the minds of lawyers—is a crucial assumption: that justice is best served by having two lawyers (or teams of lawyers) fighting one another. Each acts as an advocate for one side of the case, and an adversary to the other. Hence, the American legal system is called an *adversary* system.

Most would argue this is a good thing. There's a close analogy with sports. The underlying purpose of any sport is to benefit the participants, to give them pleasure and push them toward physical excellence. Both goals are better served when the athlete has competition. So too, in the legal realm, arguments and evidence are made stronger and better by responding to *counter*arguments and *counter*evidence. Justice and truth are best served when each side is forced to present its best case.

Of course sports serve other purposes as well: excitement for those watching, and lots of money for lots of people. But let's stay with athletics' intrinsic purposes—physical excellence and the pleasures of playing. These goals aren't sought directly. During the game the quarterback is not trying to improve his fitness, or to enjoy himself; he's trying to win. The ultimate goals of sports, pleasure and fitness, are best served by having each side pursue the *intermediate* goal of victory. Similarly, the ultimate goal of law—to see truth and justice triumph—is best served by having each side seek the intermediate goal of victory, with lawyers acting as zealous advocates and zealous adversaries. Or so we think.

Serving or Conflicting?

What *The Good Wife* shows so well—by the clarity and subtlety of its script, and by fine acting—is that the intermediate goal can conflict with the ultimate goal. This can happen in sports, too. Set aside the corruption that big money brings with it. Even in a pickup basketball game players can get so caught up that they hurt themselves and each other. As the stakes get higher, injury becomes more likely.

The rules of sports are meant to prevent these problems, and to some extent they do. The rules of our legal system have a similar purpose, and similar mixed success. Rules in both arenas are regularly re-thought. Concern about concussions is changing rules about football helmets. In the law, scandals like Enron led to tougher rules about the use of perjured testimony. The instrumental lawyerly goal of winning the case with zealous advocacy is always in danger of conflicting with the ultimate goal of bringing about truth and justice. It's the nature of the beast.

How deep is the danger? How well does competition in the courts serve justice? Actually that's not quite the question. Justice, paradoxically, is not the ultimate end of the justice system; its truly ultimate purpose is maintaining order. Civil courts resolve disputes, and doing that manages anger between citizens. Criminal courts enforce the law by meting out punishments; these in turn discourage law breaking. The connection between these ultimate results and what Alicia does is pretty indirect. Theoretically one could even say that her work is optional; other societies, after all, have reconciled neighbors and punished scofflaws quite differently: by royal fiat, sometimes, or by physical trials (letting the aggrieved parties duel one another, for instance, or trying to drown a suspected witch). But obviously none of that will do for us. We expect our courts not only to decide, but to decide fairly. Otherwise they lose our allegiance and we take matters into our own hands, with brutal results.

So now we've placed Alicia, Will, Diane, and other lawyers at the beginning of a long causal chain. They defend their clients (vigorously and inventively), and doing so, in theory, brings about justice in the courtroom. Justice in the courtroom channels anger and preserves public peace. Both links need attention.

The Advocacy-Justice Link

Start with the link between what lawyers do and what courts decide. Certainly questionable tactics abound. The Season Two episode "Cleaning House" involves a case in which several people had been crushed in a rave; the victims had probably been high on PCP. Alicia is asked how she would feel about "blaming the victim" and she replies, "How would I feel as a person? Or as a lawyer?" As a person she would hate it, obviously; but as a lawyer she is quite willing to use this strategy. If she were pressed on this, she might have given the response lawyers often do: "The other side has a lawyer, too." The assumption is that with each side energetically looking for arguments and evidence, everything relevant should come to light; the truth will out, and justice will be served.

In reality, as we all know, the resources (read money) available to each side can be vastly different. Forget O.J.— worse than the likelihood that someone guilty went free is the certainty that the innocent have been imprisoned, and sometimes executed. Money talks, far more than it should. In capital punishment, the saying goes, "Those without the capital get the punishment." This is the practical weakness in the adversary system.

The role of money could, in theory, be vastly lessened. We could, for instance, allow each side only one lawyer, salaried by the state. Personal wealth would no longer matter. Even such a radical change—politically impossible anyway— would not completely level the playing field. No two lawyers are equally skilled. Verdicts would sometimes be a result of a lawyer's ability rather than the facts. But in such a system adversarial justice, with someone working energetically on each side, would at least help balance the scales.

That sort of solution might not be possible for the American legal system. Even if it were possible, a deeper problem would persist. No one in the adversarial courtroom is directly responsible for bringing the truth to light. Each lawyer defends his or her own case, the judge makes sure the rules are followed, and the jury (when there is one) sorts out what has been presented. It is quite possible for each side to want to keep something relevant out of court, for different reasons. In the ongoing struggle between Peter and his nemesis, Glenn Childs, for example ("Hybristophilia"), some tapes are never used as evidence. Each side, in different ways, is afraid of what they would show.

Another Weak Link?

What about the link between having courts decide and the channeling of public anger? The answer's ambiguous. Most people's exposure to the American legal system is through high-profile trials like those of Casey Anthony, O.J. Simpson, and the cops who beat Rodney King. The public response to acquittal has ranged from anger to riots. Yet riots are rare, and so are violent feuds between families. (Rare, but not nonexistent). The Hatfields and the McCoys made peace, notably, after courts passed sentences of imprisonment and death. Our courts, despite all their flaws, work pretty well at keeping the peace.

The courts succeed in part because we all understand, at some level, that private vengeance is uncontrollable. Public court processes, frustrating and often unfair, are still preferable. (Another deterrent to private vengeance is simpler: the police punish it pretty effectively.) There's also the (maybe only half-conscious) understanding that everyone needs and deserves someone fighting on their side. For all the outrage when someone who's probably guilty is acquitted, we want a lawyer for ourselves should we be accused. And we want a good one.

Having no one on our side would terrify us. It would terrify us most if we were accused of a crime, and had to defend ourselves against the full power of the state. In civil cases we might not feel quite so vulnerable, especially if the other party were also on their own. Small claims courts operate that way: the disagreeing parties face one another and present their case; the judge decides. Traffic courts are often similar: no lawyers, no jury, just the accuser (police), the accused, and a judge.

In some countries many or all trials—civil or criminal, misdemeanor or felony—are handled this way. Such systems are called *inquisitorial*, and in spite of the unpleasant name, have a lot going for them. Judges in our system are supposed to be impartial referees; judges in other countries are also impartial, but unlike ours can play an active role in getting the facts, from questioning witnesses to ordering investigations. Most legal systems are hybrid, partly adversarial, partly inquisitorial. (A better name might be *investigational*.)

Resisting the State

Why then are American courts almost entirely adversarial? That they are provides *The Good Wife* with week after week of riveting drama, but that's hardly an answer. History supplies the beginning of an answer. Our country was founded in order to throw off the oppressive British government. Protecting individual liberty against the power of the state is our most basic commitment. The words *liberty* and *freedom* are thrown around constantly, in political battles and even in meaningless commercials. (7-Eleven once proclaimed "Freedom! We offer BOTH Coke and Pepsi!" Politicians' use of the word is usually worse.)

What really counts as liberty (since a choice between sodas does not)? How important is liberty? Why? Answers are deep and varied, but we all agree on this: The essence of being human includes the ability to live your own life, to make your own choices. In other words, liberty.

Some government policies support that ability, some get in the way. Political philosophy tackles those issues, and there are two important things we can learn from what it says: First, individual liberty is profoundly important; second, the state is a uniquely powerful institution and, when unchecked, a threat to liberty. Here, finally, is a clear defense of lawyerly activity: When the accused is face to face with the state, the scales should be weighted on behalf of the accused. The goal of legal advocacy is protection of the individual against the state.

This defense is very limited, though. It justifies zeal in criminal defense attorneys, but not for prosecuting attorneys, nor for either side of a lawsuit. So where do we go from here? Political philosopher David Luban reaches an almost cynical conclusion. First he makes a simple, fundamental point: The adversary system is imperfect, but so is every other system. Then he gets practical: Changing our legal system would make a true mess for a long time. Unintended consequences would have a field day. So, Luban concludes, the adversary system is justified.

But legal advocacy as part of an adversary system still raises deep ethical issues. It is objectively justified only in criminal cases. In other situations, lawyers are not so justified in doing what would be wrong for non-lawyers. Or, as Luban puts it, "professionalism can tell lawyers not to cut corners. . . . it cannot mandate them to cut throats."

At this point his cynicism kicks in. Lawyers are not going to change. Alicia, Will, and others will use cutthroat tactics whenever they will work. Like the rest of us, lawyers are paid to do effective work, not to fine tune their consciences. "Criticizing an ideology," Luban writes, "won't change the world." But we're better off with one less excuse for what we do.

Cynicism Aside . . . Possibly

The Good Wife does get many things right about lawyerly professional obligations as well as legal ethics, and it's refreshing when the firm does the difficult but ethical thing. Take an example from the Season One episode "Hi." The wife of a client suspected of murder is suddenly herself a suspect. The firm immediately separates her defense from his—each will have a different team, and the two teams will not communicate. This is what professional ethics requires. Also, in the episode

"Lifeguard" from Season One, Will discovers that an old lawyer friend of his has become corrupt. Despite the history they have together and the fact that the friend's career will be over, Will ends up exposing him for who he really is.

But in the world of *The Good Wife*—as in the real world—'legal ethics' may seem to non-lawyers to be an oxymoron. In the Season One episode "Unplugged" Eli Gold says to Alicia, "In my experience, everyone is 'that *kind*' of person": someone who will do what it takes to get what he or she wants. Alicia wavers and ponders: Is she *herself* like that? By the middle of Season Two, she tells her brother that everyone is double faced. "Even you?" he asks? "Yes," she replies. "I've grown up."

Alicia will remain conflicted, the voice of uneasy conscience in the show. It is to her credit—and that of the writers of *The Good Wife*—that she has not simply reconciled herself to the ambiguous world in which she must practice.

2
Death's Just a Click Away

JAI GALLIOTT

Alongside a comical look at Eli Gold's world of crisis management and food lobbyists, there's a powerful indictment of the US military's drone warfare practices in the Season Three episode "Whiskey Tango Foxtrot." This episode harks back to one of Season Two's best, "Double Jeopardy," where Alicia and Will work with Captain Hicks to defend a murder suspect in military court.

This time, Hicks requests that Lockhart Gardner help defend a young female soldier, Sergeant Elkins. The twist: Elkins is a drone aircraft operator who, while working out of a Nevada-based control station, killed twelve innocent Afghani civilians with a misguided missile attack. The military jury is asked to judge the accused on the merits of the law, but since the law has some pretty big holes in it, in this chapter I'm going to pass *moral* judgment on Elkins's actions and the use of these systems. I don't know what's more worrying, though: that an operator could intentionally kill civilians or that they could do so unintentionally and that many people see nothing morally questionable about waging combat this way.

In case it hasn't already clicked, the title of episode, Whiskey Tango Foxtrot," is NATO-speak for "What the fuck?" It describes what most people are probably left thinking having watched the opening scene. We see a woman's pale white hands gently punching a keyboard, and with a press of the return key, we're shown black and white footage of roads, irregular housing blocks, and palm trees. With a few jolting movements, we focus in on a pickup truck on the street. The shadows of those walking up and down it are visible on the pavement. A red circle appears around the truck and "enemy combatant 4-9-5" is scrawled next to it, as if handwritten.

On the other side of a door inscribed "Department of Defense General Counsel," a man watching a relay of the drone footage on a large screen enters the value 4-9-5 into a program running on his laptop. As he does this, those people near the truck are circled and labeled "non enemy combatant—4 adults, 1 minor." Guys in black suits huddle around the screen. They scan the area and find a large mosque, just over one hundred feet from target. As the dainty white hand grabs the joystick, the focus tightens on the truck and, as it does, a cyclist approaches. The truck explodes, destroying a nearby building and blowing the cyclist and all those within thirty feet back to the Middle Ages. Survivors flee, clearly engulfed in flames.

Apart from being highly watchable television, this is a fairly accurate portrayal of an actual drone strike, thousands of which have been conducted since the beginning of the latest round of military operations in Afghanistan and Iraq. The word *drone* encompasses a range of terms, including unmanned aerial system (UAS), uninhabited aerial vehicle (UAV), and remotely piloted vehicle (RPV).

Those used by the US military have cuddly names such as the Predator and Reaper. There are drones that can fly on their own, and there are others that are remotely controlled, as in this case. Whatever the variety, we're talking about those aircraft that fly above us without a pilot onboard and, more often than not, are capable of raining down Hellfire missiles as Zeus does lightning bolts. These systems can be operated from any place with a satellite dish and the right computer equipment, distancing soldiers from the dull, dirty, and dangerous tasks they'd otherwise have to face directly, which, of course, is why they're so well loved. Sergeant Elkins is the drone's sensor operator and, in her own words, she reads and responds to "real time, on-the-ground alterations as detected by the UAV's sensors and controls the Predator's targeting systems." In other words, she's the one that paints a big, infrared target on your back. There's also a pilot, Lieutenant Ventura. He's not a "pilot in the drone"—as Alicia suggests in confusion—but rather one based on the ground, typically sitting right next to the sensor operator.

Again, it's Elkins who's heading for confinement; after all, she was the operator that made the targeting decisions. Her commanding officer accuses her of inaccurate and unprofessional reporting as to the presence of twelve unarmed civilians, which resulted in their fiery deaths. She therefore faces twelve counts of murder, despite the fact that there must have been hundreds of civilian deaths in similar drone mishaps. In a meeting in which Alicia, Will, and Hicks provide counsel, Elkins admits that the twelve civilians were killed but denies the murder charges, explaining that there are occasional delays in the transmission of text alerts and sensor relays. She says that she received information about the presence of civilians too late to take any corrective action or abort the mission.

At this point, Hicks chimes in and states that "the transmission is logged as on time because it indicates the time it was sent, but not the time it arrived." Alicia asks whether there's anyone who can corroborate that there was a delay in the transmission alerting to the presence of civilians. "My pilot saw it, too," she claims. However, in giving testimony, Ventura claims that while there are sometimes delays in such transmissions, they didn't experience any in this instance. "Then why did the accused ignore the alert?" the prosecution asks. "Objection," Will roars. However, there's no objection on my part as it's precisely these sorts of questions that need answering if we are to determine whether drones and their operators are an intolerable moral hazard or an invaluable piece of military kit.

Morals Under the Gun

The drone case isn't one that we can deliberate on simply by appealing to our common intuitions. Like debating the legal or moral legitimacy of normal ground or air strikes (army tanks and fighter jets), deliberating on the use of drones is, at least in part, a "use of force" question. Before we can even begin to consider why Sergeant Elkins mistook these civilians for combatants and proceeded to kill them, we first have to ask ourselves: Under what circumstances is a deadly drone strike morally permissible? War is probably as close as you can get to hell on Earth. When it's unleashed, killing is not only allowed, but is often considered one's patriotic duty. This is why many people believe that war is a place where no moral constraints or laws apply.

A robe-wearing ancient philosopher named Cicero (106–43 B.C.E.) summed up this view nicely in saying that "In times of war, the laws fall mute." Yet, all is not fair in love and war, as he suggests. It turns out that there's a solid set of rules that define what is right or wrong in battle. This is especially so for the US military and litigious types like Captain Hicks and the folks at Lockhart Gardner, for whom there is the Law of Armed Conflict and International Humanitarian Law, which are supposed to regulate conduct when everything turns bad. That is, when peaceful alternatives fail. You've probably also heard of the Geneva Conventions on the Laws of War, which state that "persons taking no active part in the hostilities . . . shall in all circumstances be treated humanely." These laws generally try to help the good guys, along with the wounded, sick, and shipwrecked.

These distinctly modern Laws of War weren't just plucked out of thin air, but have developed over centuries from ancient moral and theological ideas. One of two major Indian epics, the *Mahabharata*, offers one of the first written discussions of whether the suffering caused by war can ever be justified. Of course, this discussion (between a few brothers) takes place with reference to chariots rather than drones, but the kind of vehicle that facilitated the development of what's now called *just war theory* isn't relevant here.

Parts of the Bible also tend to encourage ethical behavior in war and hint at the concept of *just cause* in suggesting that war should only be fought for certain divinely inspired reasons. Saint Augustine (354–430 C.E.) also wrote about the morality of war from a Christian perspective, warning us of the love of violence that war often engenders. However, it was Saint Thomas Aquinas (1225–1274) who gave the general outline of the just war theory that is taught to the military officers and philosophers of today. He not only discusses the justification for war, but also expands on what sorts of activities Christians ought to perform in war. Other robe-wearing scholars from the good ol' days, such as Francisco de Vitoria (1486–1546), Hugo Grotius (1583–1645), and Emerich de Vattel (1714–1767), have attempted to secularize the moral principles he proposed. Each of these scholars wanted to limit unnecessary suffering and destruction, while not impeding the waging of just war.

What we're left with today is a generally coherent set of moral laws that can be applied both to the act of going to war, *jus ad bellum*, and conduct during war, *jus in bello*. If *any* are broken, the war is said to be unjust or immoral. *Jus ad bellum* rules apply mainly to politicians and those with brass on their shoulders. It's adherence to *jus in bello* rules on which the average soldier is judged.

The two biggest rules for Elkins, as a drone operator, are those of *proportionality* and *discrimination*. Proportionality means that the suffering and devastation caused by a particular action in war should not outweigh whatever harm initiated it. In much the same way that a convenience store owner can't shoot someone for stealing a gallon of milk, one state cannot "nuke" another for stealing its citizens' cows. Discrimination (of the good kind) means that sides must also be able to distinguish combatants from civilians and respect the latter's immunity from harm. It even says that sides must respect the difference between combatants that pose a mortal threat and those that don't, such as padres or soldiers waving a white flag. Of course, some collateral damage is often considered acceptable.

In "Whiskey Tango Foxtrot," an analyst from Langley tells us that civilian deaths and damage are taken into account in the "kill chain algorithm," in which they're weighed against the strategic value of the target, to give some indication of the worthiness of an attack. The sad fact is that civilians are sometimes considered expendable, though they weren't in this case. The morally relevant question we return to, then, is why Elkins didn't adhere to these rules and what role the drone technology played in this.

Let's Blame the Bot

You've probably heard the saying that "a good workman doesn't blame his tools." Well, this phrase doesn't apply very well to pilotless aircraft, like the Predator flown by Sergeant Elkins. A carpenter can't really blame his hammer as it's a fairly neutral and mundane technological instrument, but when your tool happens to be a five-thousand-pound robotic aircraft that can carry another five thousand pounds of fuel and weaponry through the sky at two hundred miles per hour to a ceiling of fifty thousand feet, and you're not actually sitting in it, there are some factors that are going to be beyond your control. You're also likely to have to make some pretty tricky moral decisions.

It's the drone's sophisticated sensors that are the eyes and ears of cubicle warriors like Sergeant Elkins and Lieutenant Ventura. However, there are undoubtedly problems concerning situational awareness. When you have a human being physically sitting in the cockpit of aircraft, they have a much broader field of vision, which they can use to direct sensors that have a more narrow, but more focused, view. High-altitude drones can have the broader view that normally comes with a human, but it is much more difficult to extract the intelligence that the brass needs to make decisions on the ground from such an altitude. The Predator's forward looking infrared cameras, for example, typically have a forty-five-degree look-angle and minimal pan movement, meaning that the drone has to be within a few miles of the target to get a clear view. As one pilot is quoted as saying, drone warfare is "like having a knife fight in a phone booth looking through a toilet-paper tube."

We're not told whether this sort of situational awareness problem was responsible for Elkins firing on those innocent bystanders pictured above, but one might expect that once sensor technologies improve, the quality of the decisions made by drone operators will lead to more discriminate and proportionate warfare. I don't think so.

Sensors may improve somewhat, but the quality of the information provided is very much limited by the laws of physics and the complexity of the modern conflicts and battle spaces in which they're conducted. The cave systems, bunkers, and stone houses that Osama bin Laden and his terrorist buddies had been known to hide in, for example, all provide impenetrable cover from eyes in the sky. Some might go so far as to argue that even the best sensor system that we can conceive of is incapable of relaying the moral reality of the situation on ground to a sensor operator that could be sitting as much as half a world away. Even if we could give operators like Elkins access to images of the quality that they would have if they were in the field themselves, there remains a worry that they may still be lacking some sort of incommunicable information, cultural awareness, or bond with the enemy that is important to the making of discriminate and proportional lethal targeting decisions.

Killing Made Easy

Besides the largely technological problems that I've just detailed, perhaps the most important issue to arise in any discussion of drones is the ethics of killing at such long range. The pilots and sensor operators who control Predator and Reaper drones are fairly safely located thousands of miles away from the people whose lives and livelihoods they destroy. The drones they operate can fly so high and so quietly that the people they target often have no idea that they are there until they hear the sound of its missiles closing in on them.

President Obama's inflammatory joke at a recent correspondents' dinner about using a Predator drone makes this point nicely:

> The Jonas Brothers are here, they're out there somewhere. Sasha and Malia are huge fans, but boys, don't get any ideas. Two words for you: Predator drones. You will never see it coming. You think I'm joking.

With quotations like this, it's hard not to wonder whether drones make it too easy for politicians to go to war. As it applies to our case, it's hard not to think that by both physically and emotionally distancing soldiers like Sergeant Elkins from the battlefield and the consequences of their actions, drones might make it easier to kill. Despite its potential to explain unethical decision-making and incidents such as the firing of two Hellfire missiles on twelve unarmed citizens, our understanding of the distance-killing phenomenon and the moral disengagement that is often involved is at an early stage.

It is commonly accepted that human beings are brought into this world with what can only be described as a primitive survival instinct, which, without unchecked force, would lead to a certain degree of violence and savagery. In most societies, this is unacceptable and through socialization, most people (fortunately!) develop an aversion to harming and killing other human beings. But military forces have to ensure that their personnel are capable of overcoming this inhibition if they are to kill when they are ordered to do so in defense of the state and its people.

History is replete with examples of battles that were lost because soldiers bolted in panic or were otherwise unwilling to engage the enemy. Research conducted by army historian Brigadier General S.L.A. Marshall after World War II revealed that only fifteen or twenty percent of riflemen were able or willing to fire. This essentially means that a large proportion of those in the United States infantry were unwilling to take a clear shot at the enemy when they had one, or that his research was simply a bit dodgy. However, other analyses confirm the difficulties that many have in overcoming the inhibition to killing.

Another study, focusing on a group of British soldiers surrounded by tribal warriors, found that while the British opened fire at point-blank range, only one of every thirteen bullets struck with effect. It is also estimated that in Vietnam, roughly fifty thousand bullets were fired for every soldier killed in action. Elkins clearly didn't have any problem pulling the trigger, though.

Why? The self-proclaimed "killologist" (or military psychologist), Lieutenant-Colonel Dave Grossman, writes that unless one is already caught up in some sort of murderous ecstasy, indiscriminately killing people and destroying things will usually be easier when done at a distance. With every foot of distance there is a corresponding decrease in the effective portrayal of reality, however slight it may be. Lieutenant-Colonel Grossman asks us think about the relationship between the empathetic and physical proximity of the victim, the resultant difficulty and trauma of the kill, and the weapons involved, in terms of a spectrum:

- At the close end of the spectrum we have hand-to-hand combat.

- Slightly further up the spectrum we have knife and bayonet-range attacks.

- At the middle of the spectrum we find pistol, rifle, and hand grenade attacks.

- Toward the end of the spectrum there are bombing and artillery, which are often used to demonstrate the relative ease of killing at a distance.

- Yet it's only as we draw toward the very end of the spectrum that we reach drones and uninhabited warfare.

Killing at the close end of the spectrum is tremendously intense. Choking someone with your bare hands, or even stabbing someone, for instance, cannot be taken lightly; it involves a massive discharge of aggressiveness. Push-button warfare, however, is less intense and more like a video game. Therefore, it may have been relatively easy for Elkins to launch missiles at pixels on a screen. If, however, she were given a knife and told to slit the throats of women and children, I doubt she would have been willing or able to do so. It would appear that the physical separation involved provides some sort of emotional or moral buffer that makes it easier to carry out lethal actions, potentially in violation of *jus in bello* rules and the Laws of Armed Conflict.

Interviews conducted with experienced military pilots seem to confirm that the spatial and temporal distance involved in modern armed conflict has a dehumanizing effect that makes it easier to wreak havoc on the not so technologically advanced. They report that they rarely perceive the decision to kill from afar as an emotionally charged or torturous one and that they are somewhat numbed to the deaths they encounter. However, drone advocates argue that not everyone that fights from a distance is emotionally separated or morally disengaged from events on the ground.

In recounting his World War II experience, one veteran tells of his first bombing raid over Europe. As he opened his aircraft's bomb bay doors, he felt "terrible resistance, nausea, sickness, headaches, despair. He couldn't do it, but his crew chief screamed at him, 'Now! Now!' He finally pushed the button. Then he vomited." Snipers, too, are separated from their targets by some distance, but some also report feeling an intimate connection. As one sniper recalls:

> they're just targets; you try to convince yourself of that. However, imagining a man purely as a target was not easy when you had to aim specifically at him and fire and then watch him fall over, screaming and arching his back in agony.

There's a big difference between these more traditional soldiers who are located in harm's way and one that's been trained on simulators and works from a game-like console in an air-conditioned room in the United States. Even if we accept this anecdotal evidence and grant that those operating drones do develop strong emotions, there is no reason why we ought to think that they would be of the kind that would make operators less likely to cause harm. If operators develop post-traumatic stress disorder (PTSD), for example, they're just as likely to make unethical targeting decisions. Either way, drones may have psychological effects that magnify the challenges associated with discerning appropriate targets and adhering to Just War Theory.

The Good, the Bad, and the Blameworthy

So, here's what we know, or don't know: we can't really tell if Sergeant Elkins got the alert about the presence of civilians and ignored it, whether it didn't arrive at all, whether she was hampered by some other technological factor, or whether she jumped the gun as a result of some sort of moral disengagement, though they're all possibilities of moral relevance.

From our perspective, though, it seems pretty obvious that she shouldn't have fired those Hellfire missiles into the street, that the truck shouldn't be exploding, and that civilians from the nearby buildings shouldn't be running around on fire, falling to their knees as they burn. But should we hold Elkins and other (non-fictional) operators responsible for techno-logically mediated war crimes, such as that described above, and what should we make of drones, more generally?

Elkins is found guilty on all twelve counts of murder. Alicia is shocked. "She's being sent to prison because she's being scapegoated for an inaccurate drone program," she says to the judge outside the court. The judge replies "the problem with a charge of scapegoating is that it doesn't acknowledge that at a certain point, you have to hold people accountable." Of course, for the judge to say that holding her, and *only* her, accountable is a just verdict, can only be true in a legal sense. From a *moral* perspective, however, scapegoating is typically unacceptable and any blame must be fairly apportioned among those morally culpable persons who contributed to the fault or wrong in question.

Should we consider Elkins a culpable agent? That is, can we hold her morally responsible for her actions? If she did receive the alert prior to pulling the trigger, and if she did so with clear intent, then she is truly blameworthy. But suppose she were morally disengaged and had become convinced that ethical standards didn't apply in the context of her role as drone operator. Her blameworthiness is significantly reduced. She's more like a child soldier in that she doesn't really understand the full moral dimensions of what she's doing. It's almost as if her moral autonomy is in some way limited.

However, it's not as though we're without others to blame. We might, for instance, insist that the manufacturer or programmer bear some responsibility for wrongs facilitated by its technology if it had known of flaws that were not disclosed to the military forces employing them. Lockhart Gardner would then have one big product liability case on their hands! Of course, if it's decided to send the weapon into battle regardless, then it is the military force or officer who decided to deploy the system that must assume some of the responsibility. Some might even say that we should hold philosophers responsible when they join the "kill-chain" in justifying the use of drones.

But before I get blamed, I should point out another problem: there is a risk that with so many blameworthy persons, the diffusion of responsibility might encourage further unethical behavior. It opens up the "I didn't do it" response. If no one person has sole responsibility for the consequences of drone attacks, we might see more of them.

Therefore, the question of accountability and the associated technical limitations and moral disengagement which can affect adherence to just war theory, all have bearing on the broader question of whether drones are an intolerable moral hazard or an invaluable piece of kit. These weapons—which are really just an extension of earlier ranged weapons such as the crossbow, rifle, and fighter jet, and also reduce risk to soldiers like Elkins by distancing them from the battlefield and the dangers that come with it—are, indeed, an asset. The problem is that by totally removing soldiers from the battlefield, we limit their capacity to act in a morally sanctioned way. Drones are a moral hazard, but not necessarily an intolerable one. With the potential benefits they offer, it's clear there's some role for drones, but we have to give further thought to how they can be deployed and designed so as to minimize any dangers to civilians.

Meanwhile, the Jonas Brothers should probably find a bunker to hide in and quash any impure thoughts about the president's daughters.

3

The Odd Consequences of Sweeney the Snake

ROD CARVETH

The laws we come up with are themselves based in things we think are right or wrong. Why is it illegal to murder, steal, or rape? Ultimately, because it's *unethical* to murder, steal, or rape. The American legal system is influenced from a variety of ethical perspectives, one of which is the *utilitarianism* of Jeremy Bentham (1748–1832), and later John Stuart Mill (1806–1873).

For utilitarians, the consequence of an action to all affected by it is what's most important in deciding whether that action is ethical or not. If what you're about to do helps the situation, brings about pleasure, or eases pain, then it's the right decision and you should do it—if it's going to harm the situation or cause pain, then it's the wrong decision and you shouldn't do it. So, for example, given the fact that perjury not only leads to miscarriages of justice, but also to people being angry or feeling badly because of the lie, and mistrusting one another—all bad consequences— utilitarians maintain something like, "Thou shalt not commit perjury."

Utilitarianism makes sense as a good basis for a society's laws because of the fact that people are constantly interacting with one another and so they definitely need to consider the consequences of their acts upon others when making many of their decisions. Think about how society would collapse if we didn't set up laws that at least attempted to ensure good consequences or prevent bad consequences.

Despite Bentham and Mill being credited with the development of utilitarianism, the two did differ in their approach. Bentham believed that each individual act should be considered when making a moral decision, and this form of utilitarianism later came to be called *act-utilitarianism*. By contrast, Mill emphasized what later became known as *rule-utilitarianism*. While like Bentham, Mill proposed that actions are right if they tend to promote happiness and wrong if they tend to produce unhappiness, Mill distinguishes between the type of act and the context in which the act occurs. Thus, rule-utilitarianism sets up rules for types of situations, and a right action therefore must be in accord with these rules that maximize utility. These rules are generally the basic kinds you can think of such as "Thou shalt not murder, rape, steal, deceive, defraud, disadvantage" and the like.

Utilitarianism and American Law

The American legal system is adversarial in that there is a side that prosecutes people who break the law and a side that defends them. This opposition is actually a good thing since it helps to ensure that each side presents its case complete with the best possible arguments and evidence so that a fair and just outcome is achieved. It's clear that much of the motivation of the prosecution stems from a rule-utilitarian ethical perspective, which makes sense since they have the common good of the society in mind as the very reason for prosecuting the transgressor in the first place, and they want to make sure that the laws—established as general rules to guide behavior—are upheld.

One major benefit of this rule-utilitarian-based thinking for the American legal system is that it allows for the meting out of outcomes that are uniform across types of criminals. Even when a prosecutor engages in a plea bargain (reducing the charges or punishment in order to avoid the cost of a trial), she's thinking like a rule-utilitarian since she's balancing the benefit of sanctioning the legal transgressor versus the cost to the public of a trial.

The defense oftentimes operates from the act-utilitarianism perspective representing only the client, and, therefore, is going to try and obtain the greatest "pleasure" (or least punishment) for the client in *this* particular case. Ideally, the defense obtains a result where the client isn't guilty and doesn't face any punishment or, at least, faces minimal punishment. Unlike the prosecution, the defense isn't focused on *rules* to bring about the greatest utility, but the action of the client in the case. Further than this, winning a case is a benefit to the defense since notoriety and other good consequences follow, such as charging more for services. Act-utilitarian thinking also is beneficial to the US legal system since it allows for more flexibility to tailor the punishment if not to the crime, at least to the criminal.

Complicating the legal process further is that both the prosecution and defense are obligated to operate according to legal rules of procedure. Violating these rules can result in the lawyer being suspended from practice, or worse, losing the ability to practice. The pressures on both sides to follow the rules are strong, but there's a key difference. If a defense lawyer (or law firm) can't continue to provide "pleasure" for clients, the lawyer (or firm) will not be in business long. Therefore, satisfying your clients while still conforming to the rules of legal procedure can be a difficult balancing act, particularly if the client doesn't value the rules a defense lawyer needs to abide by. So, while the defense operates from the ethical perspective of act-utilitarianism, the actions it employs are bounded by the rules of legal procedure.

Serpentine, Sleazy, Sweeney?

There are a number of cases in *The Good Wife* that illustrate the tensions between these forms of utilitarianism, but the cases involving recurring character Colin Sweeney illustrate the depth and breadth of the tensions of satisfying the client while working within the rules of the American legal system. Over the first four seasons of the series, Lockhart Gardner successfully defends Sweeney in a wrongful death suit (though he actually was guilty), gets Sweeney a manslaughter deal when he kills a stalker/lover, obtains Sweeney's release so that he can provide supportive testimony in other firm litigation, and finally defends him against sexual harassment litigation while he tries to get his business back. And in each case, the firm approached Sweeney and his cases from an act-utilitarian perspective.

Sweeney (Dylan Baker) was introduced in the Season One episode "Bad" and had previously been found not guilty of murdering his wife in a notorious case that members of the firm compare to O.J. Simpson's. Sweeney is being sued by his stepdaughter, Charlotte, to keep him from inheriting his dead wife's estate. Despite Sweeney's notoriety, Will Gardner agrees to take his case because he wants Sweeney's other legal business. Diane Lockhart is less sanguine about the effect representing Sweeney will have on the firm's present clients. Will notes that they need the business Sweeney may give them because their former partner Jonas Stern walked away with a third of their clients. Will asks Alicia to be second chair in the case because her husband, Peter, had prosecuted Sweeney during his murder trial. When Sweeney greets Alicia with a handshake, he jokes in a macabre fashion, "Don't worry. I killed my wife with my other hand." Sweeney later asks Alicia if she believes that he killed his wife. She replies, "Of course."

Here the firm, or at least named-partner Will Gardner, makes a decision based on act-utilitarianism. Will doesn't appear to be completely convinced of Sweeney's innocence in his murder trial, and Alicia believes him to be guilty. In order to defend Sweeney, Will and Alicia have to argue that Sweeney is not guilty of murdering his wife, an argument that neither truly believes. Yet Will knows that his firm needs Sweeney's business, and the notoriety and money that will result from successfully defending him.

From a practical point of view, Will and Alicia have an ethical dilemma. If a lawyer knows that the client is providing false testimony that means the lawyer is suborning perjury, an offense that can lead to disbarment. In a civil trial, a client must testify; therefore, the client's lawyers must elicit testimony from the client. In this case, however, the fact that Sweeney has been found not guilty of killing his wife means that he can "truthfully" testify he did not kill his wife. Therefore, from a legal perspective, if Will and Alicia ask Sweeney questions while he is on the stand, it's not suborning perjury. Still, though eliciting testimony from Sweeney doesn't present any legal problems for the firm, it does present an ethical dilemma for Will and Alicia.

The case takes bad turn when police discover Carolyn Sweeney's skull buried in the garden at the penthouse Sweeney formerly lived in. The firm's investigator, Kalinda, discovers from the coroner that the skull contained pesticides, similar to those that could be found at a farm. Charlotte owns an organic farm that she has tried—unsuccessfully—to make into a business. Will and Alicia get Charlotte to admit on the stand that she and her mother fought over money spent on the farm. Kalinda passes the information about the skull containing pesticides on to the authorities who find the rest of her mother's remains on the daughter's farm. Charlotte is arrested, and the case against Sweeney is tossed out.

Means and Ends

Sweeney returns in the Season One episode "Hybristophilia." While at a bar with Kalinda, Alicia gets a phone call from Will who asks her to do a favor and pick up some merger papers from a client—Colin Sweeney. Alicia reluctantly goes to Sweeney's residence where she finds him in his study dressed in a bloodied robe, handcuffed to a woman on the floor dead from stabbing. Sweeney protests to Alicia that "This . . . this is not what it looks like." Sweeney claims that they had sex several times, but "this time it was different.

This time she tried to kill me." Based on this information, the firm decides to pursue a defense of *hybristophilia*, a mental condition afflicting women who are irresistibly attracted to dangerous men. (Think Bonnie in relation to Clyde.) Alicia will second chair Sweeney's defense with one of the firm's partners, Julius Cain.

Alicia later overhears Diane and Will discussing the impact of Sweeney's arrest on the impending merger. Diane laments, "The CEO's just accused of murder. Everyone'll scramble." Will responds, "Not necessarily. The buyer is motivated and money is money." The firm has an ethical conflict. On the one hand, they have a client that they are defending in a murder trial. On the other hand, they are representing his firm in a merger. The fact that he is on trial for murder could scuttle the merger, costing the firm money.

Will and Diane check with the buyers and find that the merger is still on. They call Julius in to inform him about the news. Diane reports, "If anything, Mr. Sweeney's troubles have shored up the buyers' interest." It is clear that Will and Diane, the two named partners of the firm, and Julius, an equity partner of the firm, have made the merger a priority over defending a client accused of murder. From their perspective, the partners are employing an act-utilitarian ethical position. If the merger goes through, there is more money for a firm that has just laid off several associates. While Sweeney's interests may be sacrificed in the process, he is but one person, and a person who may have gotten away with murder at that.

But there's more to this situation from the act utilitarian perspective. Given the emphasis upon bringing about good consequences, act-utilitarians *especially* argue the end of bringing about good consequences justifies the means of doing something like lying, cheating, deceiving, manipulating, or withholding information in order to bring the good about. And certainly, in the case of Sweeney who's a serpentine, sleazy SOB, sacrificing his interests to secure the merger is a no brainer, then.

Ultimately Julius and Alicia are able to secure a deal from the prosecutor for an eight-year sentence for Sweeney.

When Julius and Alicia present the deal to Sweeney, he asks to see Alicia alone. During their meeting together, Sweeney realizes that his imprisonment helps the merger. He also reveals that he did, indeed, kill his wife. Sweeney observes that his present dilemma is "Karma" for his past transgression. In the end, the merger goes through, and Sweeney, though holding a significant number of shares, is powerless to run his company. From the act-utilitarian perspective of Lockhart Gardner, the end certainly justifies the means.

The Law Is an Odd Thing

Another episode of note with Sweeney is Season Three's "Long Way Home." The episode opens with Sweeney preparing for a proxy fight to take back leadership of his company, Herald Equity, from Gerald Dresher (who assumed the reins while Sweeney was in prison). The firm is lining up support for Sweeney in return for a five-percent stake in the company. One mutual fund is withholding support, however, unless Diane can promise that there will be no more "drama" from Sweeney.

Sweeney speaks before the stockholders and just before finishing takes a question from a woman who identifies herself as Isabel Swift, an event planner at Herald Equity. She accuses him of sexual harassment. Sweeney refutes her claim: "Young lady, you know that's not true." Swift then replies, "Then how do you explain this?" Swift picks up a boy of about three years old and announces, "Meet your son, Mr. Sweeney."

The surprise announcement results in Sweeney losing the proxy vote. Consequently, Sweeney has three days to liquidate his shares unless Lockhart Gardner can win an injunction overturning the proxy vote. In order to win the injunction, the firm has to prove that Sweeney isn't the father of the child, and that Dresher and Swift colluded to commit a fraud in order to sway the proxy vote. On the stand, Sweeney declares that he never had sex with Swift. Kalinda finds out from a waitress that Sweeney and Swift had come out of a men's room with "their clothes half off." When confronted with Kalinda's findings, Sweeney admits that he had "oral sex" with Swift, but that it wasn't "real sex." At this point, Alicia knows Sweeney has perjured himself.

Alicia consults with Will about the perjury. According to Will, Alicia is not in trouble if the perjury occurred without her prior knowledge. However, Alicia can't continue to elicit testimony from Sweeney, or else she would knowingly be suborning perjury. Alicia then asks if she can use the perjured testimony in cross-examining another witness. Will replies she can use the perjured testimony because she must represent the client to the best of her ability: it's part of the record and she didn't know it was perjured testimony at the time of the perjury when it happened. Alicia observes, "The law is an odd thing." Will warns Alicia, however, that if the opposing counsel puts Sweeney back on the stand, Alicia has to be careful not to elicit further perjured testimony.

Alicia's observation about the law being "an odd thing" certainly applies in this case. Her client has lied. Yet, though ethically she might be obligated to alert the court and the opposing counsel about the lie, legally she isn't required to. In this case, taking the perspective of act-utilitarianism means she doesn't act. Beyond that, legally she is required to provide the best representation she can for her client, even to the extent of using the perjured testimony to her client's advantage.

After a few more courtroom encounters, near the end of the episode Sweeney shows up at Lockhart Gardner with his son and Swift. His legal team is stunned when he announces that he and Swift have reached a "sensible accommodation." Swift acknowledges she was impregnated by "unconventional means" and further acknowledges Dresher's involvement in the attempt to unfairly win the proxy battle. Sweeney leaves with Swift, his new son, and his company. The firm is left with the knowledge that two perjurers have just made a deal that the firm is signing off on. For Lockhart Gardner, the ethical position here is again act-utilitarian: the end justifies the actions (and inactions) they took.

Crossing Lines?

Over the course of the series, the lawyers at Lockhart Gardner have dealt with a number of ethical dilemmas. In fact, Will Gardner served a six-month suspension for inappropriate use of client funds. The episodes involving Colin Sweeney illustrate a firm that will definitely approach an ethical line, and may even appear to cross it at times. Because the firm employs the perspective of act-utilitarianism, the firm's ethical compass is—shall we say—flexible. The firm represented a client in a wrongful death case they believed was guilty; failed to disclose incriminating evidence in the client's second murder trial; used that client for financial gain in another civil suit; allowed a client who had already committed perjury to continue his perjury on the stand; and allowed two perjurers to file an affidavit with the court asserting fraud by another party. All of these actions maximize pleasure for the client and the firm in an act-utilitarian way.

Having admitted to killing his wife, and probably killing a woman he had an affair with, by the end of the fourth season of *The Good Wife* Colin Sweeney is a free man, back in charge of his firm, and a father to boot. It's counter-intuitive results like this that cause us to question whether act-utilitarianism should be the basis for our decision making. In any event, it makes for great television!

II

Why She's the
Good Wife

4
How to Love When You're a Good Wife

CÉLINE MORIN

When a video of your husband and a prostitute ends up on TMZ, you tend to reconsider your love life. Ultimately this forty-year-old mother of two, who's been publicly humiliated by the infidelities and corruptions of her politician husband and who has to go back to work under the supervision of her former, and quite handsome ex-boyfriend (for whom she obviously still has feelings) mixes all kinds of love patterns colliding with aspirations of independency. Alicia Florrick's life isn't easy, and her love life is simply chaotic hell.

But *The Good Wife* is about something bigger than a woman going through a public humiliation and having to go back to work. The story is basically about a good woman, a good wife, who's tired of being walked all over, goes against the grain, and rebels. She's rebelling quietly and properly because she's a well-educated white, upper-class woman but still, she's rebelling, people!

She's adopting a new independent lifestyle; she's dealing differently with her love life. *The Good Wife* is an amazing show for a lot of reasons but it's particularly innovative inasmuch as Alicia brings together the very glamorous topic of love (haaa, love . . .) and the apparently not-so-much glamorous topic of feminism. Surprisingly the excitement isn't always where we think it'd be: Alicia's discovery of feminism, with the help of her activist boss Diane Lockhart, often makes sparks fly and brings a lot of pleasurable uprisings within traditional patterns.

2,400 Years Ago

Traditionally, Greek philosophers have distinguished three big types of love: Agapé, Eros, and Philia. As philosopher Neera Badhwar puts it, Agapé is a universal love "independent of the loved individual's fundamental characteristics," it's the love of people beyond their qualities or their flaws. Through the Christian values, it became the kind of love God has for humans, and humans for God; a brotherly love that should concern anyone unconditionally ("Love your enemies," says the Bible [Matthew 5:44], without any expectation of reciprocity or any kind of appraisal or motivation. Not easy.)

Then, there's Eros. Eros is tricky because it has become *erotic, eroticism,* a sexual affair; a matter of the flesh. But in Greek mythology, Eros is one of the most powerful Gods, the God of Love, one of the primary forces of the cosmos. To fully understand Eros, the main subject matter of Plato's *Symposium*—an entire dialogue devoted to love philosophically of course—we should make a small detour via something Plato called the "Realm of Forms."

Before we incarnated into the material humans that we are, we were souls, living in a celestial world with Gods and Forms. We all know what a God is, but what's a Form? It's a non-material and perfect essence; it's the fundamental of things. For example, if we're talking about the Form of Beauty, note the caps: we're talking about Beauty in its whole, substantial idea. The Form of Beauty *is* Beauty. According to Plato, we got a glimpse of those perfect Forms and although we don't have access to it anymore (they're in the skies, we're stuck on Earth) we still have some memories of them that are sometimes activated by something or someone.

In Plato's *Symposium*, Socrates went on to say that when we love someone it's not because this person is fabulous, amazing, and extraordinary but because he or she has something that reminds us of Beauty we contemplated in our previous life. People have beauty that comes from Beauty. We carry a bit of the divine.

Therefore to love someone is to love the celestial in him, it's to love something bigger that reflects in him: the love of somebody because he's unique and individual doesn't really exist in Greek philosophy, pretty much like it doesn't exist in Agapé. The idea that the love of two individuals for each other draws upon much larger forces survives in contemporary practices and representations of love. We'll see how Alicia struggles when it comes to forgiving in accordance with Christian values or when it comes to having a relationship with Will without damaging larger structures like family or work.

Let's go back to Eros, which Socrates precisely defines as the love of Beauty. The sexual attraction one person feels for another is in fact an imperfect reaction to his or her beauty, in which lies something bigger. Socrates wishes this little interaction be developed into the love of Beauty itself with the help of contemplation, which means that even the sexual desires that we now wrongly consider crude are in fact the first step toward a spiritual love.

Like Agapé, Eros is an unconditional love but it responds to the loved one's particular qualities; it's the affection for a human being according to what he or she can provide. Unlike Agapé then, we appraise people and afterwards, depending on what we find, we love them. Eros sees the qualities in people and appraises their value accordingly; Agapé *creates* value in people because they are linked to Beauty.

Finally, Philia is an affectionate love that also responds to a person's qualities, this major and common component between Eros and Philia leading contemporary philosophers to diminish the distinction between them but in our case, given the first half of Season Three and its depiction of Alicia and Will's affair, we can't ignore the importance of sexual desires in *The Good Wife*. And since there's no sex in Philia, I will preserve the distinction here, keeping in mind that they are indeed quite similar.

This threefold definition of love is at work in *The Good Wife* but never in an easy manner; first, because those three types are entangled in more contemporary models of relationships like romanticism, passion, or eroticism. They might be contradictory but they're not mutually exclusive. For example, if there's clearly Agapé between Alicia and Peter (how do you continue to unconditionally love someone who cheated on you, and lied to you?), it doesn't stop them from some erotic, even torrid, reunion on the washing machine that Christian values wouldn't approve of ("Taking Control"). There's never a simple diagram or unique links between abstract ideas and concrete applications and practices, much less in love and very much less on television shows where the complexity of relationships is so important for the stories (a quick look at any soap opera with the 'sister-who's-really-your-mother GASP!' or the 'boyfriend-who's-actually-your-brother GASP! again' is striking).

So let's try and unravel this mess.

Sleeping with Prostitutes

When it comes to love, the idea that there's something bigger than the couple is widespread. It's been in Plato's philosophy: people are looking at Beauty when they fall in love with someone.

It's also at the core of romanticism. According to this love pattern that was born at the end of the eighteenth century and that still follows us today, the loved ones are supposed to fill a gap in each other's hearts. They do so by combining their souls; that's the 'soul mate' concept. Like Eros, romantic love overwhelms individuals so much that there's very little room left for personal goals, which is why it has difficulties surviving nowadays: in societies that are more and more individualized, people tend to be less and less romantic. That's also why Alicia will distance herself from this pattern; emancipation includes individualization that itself implies both more freedom and new ways of loving. It's true that romanticism is partly outmoded and *The Good Wife* provides us some flashbacks that illustrate perfectly these romantic dreams and their obsolescence.

In "You Can't Go Home Again," Alicia and Peter throw a party. Alicia's wearing a sunny dress and a pearl necklace and Peter entertains their friends with his wife's latest story. He's obviously proud of her, they're laughing, and the whole scene is filmed with a camera blur, suggesting happy days and nostalgia. *The Good Wife* works so much on subtleness and restraint that I can't believe this depiction of marriage isn't voluntarily a caricature. A *pearl* necklace, really?

Anyways, the nuclear family is doing great and, cherry on the cake, we learn that Alicia is even secretly envied by one of her female neighbors and alleged "friends" (the same one that will turn her back on her a few weeks later); that, in fashionable districts, is the ultimate sign of success. Therefore the upcoming revelations about her husband's infidelities are more than just a public humiliation: it actually represents romanticism's failures. Her marriage, that is the social structuration of her romantic hopes, led her to subjection and disgrace. She wanted to have a calm home and she ended up on tabloids. In other words, Eros, the unconditional love of Beauty, the appraisal of people, the source of romanticism, has failed.

How's Your Agapé Doing?

From then, Agapé takes over. Once Peter's infidelities are revealed, he repeatedly calls for forgiveness. "When are you going to forgive me, for Christ's sakes?", he asks (very indecently). Consequently, Alicia's Agapé towards him is constantly challenged by his actions and how little she knows of them. "If you want me to forgive you, I need to know what I am forgiving you for," she answers ("Stripped").

During the whole series, Alicia hesitates between following Agapé principles and forgiving her husband, believing that he will behave better—that's the universal love of Agapé beyond people's flaws and mistakes—and the need to know what he has done in order to appraise his actions and forgive him thanks to this knowledge. Over the episodes, she chooses the latter as she'll stop being this carefree housewife who blindly trusts her man because of the wedding ring that unites them.

In the episode "Boom" of Season Two, Alicia tells Peter that, "It's over. Us. Me caring. Me actually thinking that you're changing." When he tries to convince her that he *is* changing, she doesn't believe him: "No, you're not. You want to think you are so you can go back to what you did before." Peter then asks for the loving kindness he used to get from Alicia. "Then, help me. Help me. If you're right, help me." Her answer, "No," is final and marks the difficulties of Agapé.

Why does she abandon Eros, Agapé, and marriage? Because she realizes that her union with Peter was mostly to Peter's benefit. It's no coincidence that he's the one who wants "everything to go back to normal" ("Pilot"); he was the privileged one in the relationship. He had the career, the good wife, the children, money, and success. But, he had someone to thank for all this and, as it unfortunately happens all too often, he didn't quite realize this before he lost it. Alicia was doing all the work at home, she was supportive of him both in private and in public, and that enabled and empowered him to succeed.

She gave Peter something extremely valuable: the (accurate) image of a steady family and a sustainable aura. People must have thought, "Wow, if he can get such a good wife, he must be a good man." The local Democratic Chair sums it up well: "Without her, Peter is just a John who overpaid for a prostitute. With her, he's Kennedy" ("Closing Arguments").

Plato Meets Gloria Steinem

Bill Clinton, Dick Morris, Eliot Spitzer, and more recently Anthony Weiner and Dominique Strauss-Kahn, the list goes on and on. As *Good Wife* co-creator Michelle King said in an interview to BitterLawyer, "there had been this waterfall of these kinds of scandals. I think they're all over our culture. And there was always this image of the husband up there apologizing and the wife standing next to him." Add to this that most of those women are lawyers and you've got your-

self a *Good Wife* scenario. Indeed in the series the allusion
to those public scandals aren't long to come. From the pilot,
Diane connects the dots and states clearly that the movement of women's emancipation will work at the core of Alicia's life transition: "Men can be lazy, women can't," she says.
"And I think that goes double for you: not only are you coming back to the workplace fairly late but you have some very
prominent baggage." Pointing at a picture of Hillary Clinton
and her, she continues: "But hey, if she can do it, so can you!"

Feminism depicted by the Kings goes beyond a deceived
wife going back to work, it doesn't only say, "Hey look, women
can work! Who knew?" Alicia becomes an independent
woman thanks to her work, yes, but she is also making some
changes in her love life by bringing together thoughts about
love patterns and feminist perspectives. She's fascinating because we're witnessing a shift in her life that echoes the
major social changes of the last decades, a shift from her
bourgeoise identity to an independent lifestyle she would've
never taken on her own—and that she wouldn't give up for
anything anymore.

Alicia's tasted freedom and it might not be easy to get and
to defend but she likes it too much to go back to doing house-
work. That's why she keeps saying indifferently to Peter or
to Will, "I like work. I like working here" ("Heart"), "I'm really
proud of the work I've done here" ("Unplugged"), and when
Peter goes back into politics to be the State's Attorney again,
she agrees to help him on two conditions: that the kids stay
away from the campaign and that she continues to work
("Running").

But look closely: her work is a *consequence* of a bigger
transition that involves her marriage, her friends, her
lifestyle, her love life; her discovery of what feminism can
bring her is at the junction. Alicia's thrown away her cardi-
gans and headbands. It's time for professional clothes and
briefcases. Suit up, women!

It's also no coincidence that the greatest enemy she encounters on her way is her mother-in-law Jackie, who stands
by her son at all costs and who, above all, reproaches Alicia

for not doing the same. Those two women are separated by a huge feminist wave that took place in the 1970s and that has encouraged women to no longer be irreducibly linked to their husbands. That's a matter of generation even Eli Gold doesn't ignore: when Jackie tells him that Alicia "won't swallow her pride, she won't forgive Peter, it's easier to leave him," he dismisses her view out of hand: "Jackie, it's not the Fifties" ("In Sickness"). Her disapprobation of Alicia's work and new lifestyle is above all disapprobation of feminism and its consequences on the marriage institution, revealed here as profoundly controlling of Alicia.

Show Me the Plan!

Alicia doesn't stay single very long as for months Will has watched her and waited for her to be free. Their story, a classic "What if?", works on two levels: the realities of their up-and-down, of what they call their "bad timing" ("Closing Arguments"), and the descriptions each one makes of their history. What if you'd ended up with me, Alicia, rather than with Peter? What would've happened? As if she wanted to convince herself, Alicia tells him that "if it had been different, at Georgetown, if . . . if it had been us and not Peter, we would've lasted a week. It's romantic because it didn't happen. If it had happened, it would have just . . . been life" ("Doubt"). Their story contains a huge blank that can be filled with all the possibilities; Alicia and Will are about failures and most of all they're about lack.

Socrates too had a good story about love and lack. It goes to how Eros, the God of Love, was born. To celebrate the birth of the Goddess of Beauty Aphrodite, the Gods had a feast. Porus, God of Expediency, fell asleep in the garden and was joined by Penia, Goddess of Poverty; together they conceived Eros. Son of a poor, he is characterized by the absence. Therefore in Greek philosophy, love is about desire, and desire itself is about the lack of something or somebody.

We believe that we'll be truly happy when we possess the soul we love but according to Socrates, it's the opposite: once we get what we want, love vanishes. We can only love people who are not really there or people whom we don't really have; consequently, love does exist but is never truly achievable. This is how Alicia sees Will's love towards her when she says "It's romantic because it didn't happen." You love me because you never really got me and you still don't. The minute we're together, those romantic feelings will disappear.

The void Alicia left in Will's life could explain why he desires her, thus why he loves her, and it's filled with reveries and projections of what the relationship could've been and could still be. Throughout the series there's constantly this conflict between on the one hand his romantic ideas and big speeches and on the other hand her down-to-earth conception of love. When he's about to declare his love to her, in a scene that has become famous, she stops him with pragmatic requests: "Show me the plan. I get the romance. I need a plan. If you want to cut through all that noise, then show me a plan. Poetry is easy. It's the parent-teacher conferences that are hard." Later, he'll get back to her with the opposite of what she asked, a big and romantic declaration that dismisses rational thinking: "You wanna know my plan? My plan is I love you, okay? I've probably loved you ever since Georgetown." This is all very nice but it still doesn't tell us who's gonna do the chores.

Once Bitten, Twice Shy

Alicia's been hurt by the romantic dreams she once threw herself in. She learned how they could hide relationships of domination; she prefers with Will a relationship based on Eros and Philia that, as the Socratic and Platonic definitions specify, aren't simply of a sexual kind. Eros and Philia are a response to an individual's specific qualities and beauty— even if the insistence on the erotic dimension of their affair isn't innocent; it is indeed a big part of their relationship.

Alicia has killed Prince Charming and given up romantic reveries. She now has an unidealistic perspective on love that's embedded in what Anthony Giddens calls a 'pure relationship'. If romanticism were the love pattern that corresponds to Alicia and Peter, the 'pure relationship' would be Alicia and Will's. It's a relationship of "sexual and emotional equality" that refutes the traditional structures because they usually profit men at women's expense; gender roles tend to assign women to household tasks and men to public affairs.

A relationship like Alicia and Will's has two main and interrelated elements: a love that opposes the 'forever' of romanticism and a 'plastic sexuality' that's disconnected from reproduction and aims at sexual fulfillment. With their bad timing, Alicia and Will indeed don't fall within the scope of 'forever' love but they do have a fulfilling sexuality (remember the erotic opening of Season Three?).

More importantly the main ingredient of a 'pure relationship' is the appraisal and respect of the partner's characteristics, implying reciprocity, equality, and independence. That's what Alicia and Will have during the short time they are together: there's no jealousy that plagues the relationship, there's no ultimatum, there are no dysfunctional behaviors because they *respect* each other's desires, hopes, and ambitions.

The Good Wife Is Learning to Be a Bad Girl

If the 'pure relationship' is such a great pattern, why do they break up, then? What holds Alicia back from a successful relationship with Will are traditional structures, the remainders of her old life: her children. As she says to her brother Owen when he suggests she call Will, "I have kids. I am a parent and I have to stop being irresponsible. I'm married." Then, only then, does she say she doesn't think she's in love with Will ("What Went Wrong").

This sequence seems to say that she doesn't even give this relationship a chance because she wants to do "the right thing." Owen, who repeatedly appears to enlighten us on Alicia, tells her: "You think society is disintegrating. You don't want to get divorced 'cause everyone is divorcing. You're like that person on the *Titanic* who won't leave their room because they're afraid of being rude" ("Breaking Fast"). It's hard to know what Alicia feels for Will because she's mostly a nonverbal person and it's even worse when it comes to close relationships. But as we've known her for some years now we've come to understand one apparently paradoxical thing: she's a feminist in an upper-class environment. She has traditional values that, as Owen puts it, make her stay on the *Titanic* but at the same time she's an independent woman who wants fulfillment, professional and private fulfillment.

For now, Alicia is still trapped in her old life that she considers bigger than her will—and than her and Will. We can imagine that she'll be able to have a steady (and pure) relationship with Will once she's fully emancipated from these remains. The Season Three cliffhanger episode "The Dream Time," might be a first step: Peter has bought their old house and is about to have dinner with their kids. Zach, the oldest, asks his mother to stay with them, "No one will think it means anything. Just have some pizza. Then you can go". She refuses, goes out but hesitates on the doorstep.

On the one hand, Peter, Zach, and Grace seem to have fun; this nice picture reminds her of the good old times but is at the same time quite out of date. After what she has been through and what she has built these last three years, this is a window on the past, tempting but unreal. On the other hand, she sees her car that would bring her home to her work and her loneliness, but also to her independence and freedom.

This is a test; Alicia has to resist the temptation of the past and accept that she needs to leave it behind her. This doesn't mean that she would lose her children, but that specific era, those specific dynamics of a family that's made of 'Daddy, Mommy, Big Boy, and Little Girl', are over. Furthermore the fact that Peter and the kids are able to have fun without her means that she can indeed move on without destroying her family—whose steadiness, of course, doesn't depend exclusively on their mother. Just as Peter wasn't needed every moment of the day for the family to be happy, she no longer has to be there all the time. However Alicia suffers from Mommy Syndrome: she has trouble dealing with the fact that people can live without her supervising everything.

We could say that this is simply another dynamic, another way of living, but for someone who used to be needed every day it's rather a revolution—and a big hurt to the ego. We can imagine that once she understands that the love she has for her children, and the love she still has for Peter, won't disappear because she becomes an independent woman, once those fears go away, it'll free space for a new relationship in agreement with her new identity with Will.

5
Saint Alicia and the Burden of Care

KATHLEEN POORMAN DOUGHERTY

Alicia Florrick has guts, composure, and a keen intellect (not to mention her kickass looks and great sense of style). Alicia is also a distinctly morally appealing character. We root for her because her guts and sharp wit are accompanied by the sense that she's kind, decent, and caring. She exhibits a warm and inviting kind of morality that makes us want to like her and even to be like her. She's not called Saint Alicia for nothing!

How does Saint Alicia shape up in the light of traditional moral theories? These theories treat morality as composed of universal principles that apply to everyone, everywhere, equally. Moral thinking according to these principles is impartial and neutral. One of the most famous advocates for this kind of moral theory is Immanuel Kant (1724–1804). As Kant describes it, morality is a system of universally binding commands, or what he called *categorical imperatives*, that we as rational beings can come to understand strictly through reason.

One version of Kant's categorical imperative says that an action is morally acceptable if it would be reasonable to think that everyone else should act the same way in similar circumstances. The idea of this rule is to prevent us from making exceptions for ourselves. It's only okay for me to do it if it would also be okay for you or everyone else to do it too. In other words, we should behave in ways that we expect that everyone should behave. In formulating morality in this way, Kant's focus is on making morality rational and objective.

Emotions and feelings are to be dismissed as morally irrelevant. The problem with emotions and feelings, so far as Kant is concerned, is that they're unreliable. My emotions, for example, might cause me to behave in ways that are morally acceptable, but depending on the emotions I experience, they might also lead me astray. Kant understands emotions to be more like passions that can overcome us without any control or justification. In acting morally, then, we should distance ourselves from our feelings and our emotional ties. We should aim for reasoning that comes from a neutral and objective perspective.

Lawrence Kohlberg (1926–1987) is a famous psychologist known for his theory of moral development. Kohlberg's theory distinguishes six distinct and consecutive stages of moral development. His stages were determined through interviews with boys of a variety of ages and developmental stages. The boys were presented with moral dilemmas and their responses were then categorized with respect to developmental stage.

The earliest stage involves a simple desire to please an authority figure.

The middle stage reflects the recognition of authority and socially accepted moral rules.

The highest stage encompasses being able to reason on the basis of individually adopted rational moral principles.

At this stage, the subjects are able to identify universally accepted moral rules and apply them from an objective and neutral perspective. Kohlberg's *justice ethic*, as it has come to be known, takes the primary concept to be fairness and ties moral development to an understanding of rights and responsibilities. In this highest stage, Kohlberg's theory looks a lot like Kant's categorical imperative.

Blind Justice?

This objective perspective is often considered the central role of the judge or even of justice itself. We see just such a claim to neutral moral reasoning in the Season One episode "Infamy" when Duke Roscoe arrives in Judge Abernathy's court. Roscoe, the slimy conservative television personality, has been accused of causing the suicide of a young mother through his aggressive tabloid commentary. When Roscoe finds himself in front of the famously liberal Abernathy, he makes a meager attempt at "playing the ref" saying, "All I want is a fair shake, even though I would imagine our politics are night and day."

This is a savvy move. Roscoe may be creepy, but he isn't stupid. He has effectively called into question Abernathy's ability to behave as an ideal (and neutral) moral agent. Equally savvy, Abernathy easily responds that his court is a "blind court" and that he will "endeavor to be fair." In other words, Abernathy claims that he's quite capable of reasoning in the ways that Kant suggests we should. And according to Kohlberg, Abernathy might just as well have claimed to be fully morally developed!

Critics of both Kant and Kohlberg question whether such objectivity is even possible in quite the strong way suggested by this understanding of morality. It's not obvious that Abernathy—or any judge in the real world—is able to be as blind as he suggests. Diane even questions this kind of objectivity in the Season One episode "Stripped," suggesting that when new judges render verdicts they tend to veer to the opposite of their own personal views in an attempt to demonstrate that they are unbiased. This wouldn't be demonstrating moral objectivity anyway—just a desire to appear unbiased. Our daily lives are complex, and we more often than not consciously *and* *unconsciously* experience the world as fully situated human beings, with all the baggage that carries with it.

Making Connections

If objectivity is what full moral development looks like, it sure doesn't describe what we find appealing about Alicia.

No doubt she's as capable as anyone else of this kind of moral reasoning (she surely couldn't have gotten through law school without it), but it's not what makes us admire her. She's not known as Saint Alicia for her objective moral judgments or her neutral moral perspective. She doesn't appeal to clients because she maintains a detached and rational perspective. Clients want her exactly because they don't expect her to be neutral. They expect her to be fully and completely engaged in them. They think she will understand them and their situation. Even clients who don't know enough to request Alicia find themselves benefiting from her abilities to identify with them.

Consider when Alicia and Kalinda are interviewing Jennifer Lewis for Alicia's first case in the pilot episode. It's a pro bono case in which Jennifer has been accused of killing her husband in a murder disguised as a carjacking. When Jennifer questions how she's going to go on, Alicia gives her very practical advice: take it one day at a time; shower, nap, and avoid the television; go through the superficial actions of putting on nice clothes and make-up. When Jennifer asks if it ever gets any easier, Alicia responds tellingly: "No, but you do get better at it."

Alicia speaks from experience. She doesn't dismiss Jennifer's concerns or try to remain detached. She allows herself to identify with Jennifer, which also allows Jennifer to feel more trust. Alicia makes it known that she has experienced similar strain in her own life. She draws on her own experience to make Jennifer feel better. This is the first of many instances in which we see that Alicia's strength comes partly from her ability to make connections, to identify with people, and to build relationships with them.

When Alicia engages with people, whether they are clients, friends, or colleagues, she engages with them as full, complete, and complex human beings. She doesn't aim for detachment; she aims for connection. In the Season One episode "Home" when Kenny, the son of a former Highland Park friend, comes to see her in the office needing legal help, she doesn't dismiss him. She takes the time away from the office and drives him all the way home. She does this even after the firm has just impressed upon the staff the importance of billable hours. In explaining to his mother why she has done so, she says, "A boy I saw grow up asked for my help, and his mother used to be a friend." She responds to him based upon her relationship with him and his mother, and their relationship has altered the way she sees her moral obligation and her moral priorities.

Moral Alternatives

As a research assistant for Kohlberg, Carol Gilligan began her work as an ethicist and moral psychologist, but her own work had one significant difference: she focused primarily on female subjects. Women had typically performed relatively poorly on Kohlberg's tests of moral development. They tended to seem stuck in lower stages, rarely exhibiting the objective moral reasoning and the focus on justice that Kohlberg expected.

Gilligan saw in her female subjects not moral deficiency but a totally different framework for moral reasoning. The women weren't inadequate in comparison to Kohlberg's male subjects—they just weren't approaching moral problems in the same way. Their responses didn't fit Kohlberg's stages at all. But that didn't mean they weren't just as morally sophisticated! They were simply reasoning *differently*. Their moral approach reflected different concerns and considerations.

Insofar as men and women still have radically different experiences, it should be no real surprise that their moral reasoning is also different. If moral reasoning grows out of our shared experience and we experience the world in different ways, then our moral reasoning should be expected to reflect that difference. In the 1970s when much of this research was being done, the differences between men's and women's lives were even more distinct. Gilligan's subjects, for example, included a pool of men attempting to avoid the draft as well as a pool of women trying to decide whether to have abortions. These are radically different kinds of moral experiences.

Both are significant and morally important, but they would likely cause the men and women to consider very different factors.

Even now, women's work is often distinctly different from that of men. Women remain predominantly responsible for childcare, for the management of the household and for the care of elderly parents. Alicia, for example, gave up her career in law after two years to care for her children as a stay-at-home mother and political wife. As she puts it herself, she did Peter's laundry and cleaned his house for fifteen years. Even outside the household, women are more likely to be employed in different sorts of labor. Traditionally "pink collar" jobs, such as secretarial work, childcare, teaching, and nursing remain fields that are mostly a female labor force.

A Care Ethic

For theorists like Gilligan, women's radically different experiences prompt an alternative moral approach, one less focused on objectivity and justice and more focused on care and relationships. In looking at her experimental data carefully and assessing its implications, Gilligan developed her own theory of moral development that reflected these more typically feminine approaches to moral reasoning.

Gilligan's stages form the basis of what we now call a *care ethic*. Her theory takes caring rather than fairness as the primary moral concept. It endorses narrative and contextual thinking as the resolution to moral dilemmas, and emphasizes relationships as a primary moral good. In Gilligan's care ethic, the most fully developed moral individual is one who can balance needs for caring between the self and others. She also recognizes herself as an important object of care, but strives always to avoid exploitation and harm. This is radically different from Kohlberg's justice ethic, focused on objectivity and fairness. But it also sounds a lot more like the Saint Alicia we know and love!

Nothing in all this research on moral development was intended to suggest that all men reason according to a justice ethic and all women reason according to a care ethic, or even that any one person must always adopt the same approach. Gilligan describes the care ethic and the justice ethic as two moral orientations that we can shift between depending on the circumstances. Even so, she demonstrates that women more frequently adopt the care ethic than men.

Other feminists, such as Nel Noddings and Sara Ruddick, make even stronger claims. Nel Noddings argues that moral approaches that focus on relationships and care are morally preferable to those based upon justice and fairness, and that this approach ought to permeate our educational approach. Sara Ruddick makes mothering the focus of her work and builds a moral approach based on the maternal experience. She claims that there are distinct virtues that arise through the process of mothering, and that these virtues, if brought into the public realm, can provide the groundwork for a moral approach that focuses on peace and pacifism. According to such feminist thinkers, Alicia's moral approach, with its focus primarily on individuals and their particular needs, makes her morally *better* not just morally different!

I Care More

Alicia demonstrates the ideal instance of a caring agent in her relationships with most of her clients—except perhaps Colin Sweeney! She shows care and attentiveness to their needs, she connects with them as the particular individuals that they are and in this way earns their trust. Alicia is not only a better person because of her caring approach: she's a better lawyer.

When Kenny is charged with felony murder in the Season One episode, "Home," his father wants to bring in another much more experienced lawyer. In telling Kenny's father why she will be a better lawyer for his son, Alicia appeals to her personal relationship with Kenny saying, "I guarantee you that I care a lot more about your son than he does. Kenny will get the best defense." The implication is that her attachment to him will make her more invested in him and thus she will defend him better. And Kenny gets an out-standing defense.

Alicia's colleague Cary Agos would have been perfectly willing to plead out Kenny's case. It's only Alicia's invest-ment in Kenny as an individual, someone for whom she cares, that keeps him out of prison. Without her willing-ness to believe in his innocence and consider every possi-bility, he would have been at the mercy of a plea bargain. Admittedly, the fact that Alicia knew all the contextual de-tails of Kenny's life gave him a better defense. Kenny was not just another client; he was the recipient of Alicia's car-ing attention. Perhaps this is evidence that we should more strongly advocate for connections, context, and the impor-tance of emotional attachments in moral reasoning, not only in women, but in men as well.

In taking on Kenny's case, Alicia also asks to have some-one else serve as first chair in an attempt to provide a buffer between her and his parents, to ease the relationship. This certainly wasn't necessary. They haven't been very invested in easing their relationship with her. As we learn earlier in the episode, Kenny's mother was both Alicia's first friend in Highland Park and the first to stop talking to her when the scandal broke. Giving up first chair is failing to take the glory that she needs in a competition with Cary. She is giving up what would be in her self-interest to protect relationships. Her approach to this whole case is likely in contrast to the young lawyer she was in her first position where she clocked the highest billable hours. Now billable hours are secondary to relationships. Perhaps she has become a more fully devel-oped caring moral agent.

Burnout

In the pilot episode, Kalinda very pointedly tells Alicia that if she identifies with too many clients she'll burn out. Though Alicia dismisses the apparent criticism, we soon see that there's an element of truth in what Kalinda says. Caring does become a distinct moral burden for Alicia.

Her frustration becomes readily apparent in the Season One episode "Infamy." Alicia has been working tirelessly on the Duke Roscoe case and has just returned to her office after once again being the one to manage the client. No sooner does she get to her office than she finds David Levy saying that he is "borrowing her" to help with a divorce client. In a burst of frustration, Alicia vents to Kalinda that she is tired of always being the one to hand-hold the clients. Kalinda explains, rightly enough, that it's not a conspiracy but just that Alicia is good at it. This isn't enough, however, to make it feel more justified to Alicia. And she's right. The fact that she's good at it shouldn't make it more often her burden. She's probably good at it because she's had a lot more experience with similar circumstances in the rest of her life.

Caring is dependent on the ability to put yourself in someone else's position, to understand how others experience the world and to make sense of what would constitute a caring response. In many instances, this ability grows out of experience. If others did more of it, they'd likely be better at it too.

A double bind is apparent here. Because Alicia seems to approach morality from a caring perspective and connects particularly well with people, she is expected to do more of the caring labor. Insofar as she does more of the caring labor, others take the glory or at least the other tasks that get more recognition. The fact that she is good at expressing compassion and care and making emotional connections means that she gets less of the more traditionally rewarding work. Not only does she potentially get less of the traditionally rewarding work, she may also get less recognition for the work she does.

Alicia recognizes caring as important and wants to be the kind of person who cares. She seems to identify clearly with this moral approach. In the Season One episode, "Painkiller," Alicia is defending a doctor charged with the death of a young football player from an oxycodone overdose. As the doctor is facing jail time and the loss of his medical license, Alicia expresses to Kalinda her guilt over the fact that she doesn't care, that she just wants his problems out of the office, saying, "What does that say about me?" In this case, she is experiencing her own lack of care as a personal moral failing. She represents here a moral dilemma. She thinks of caring as an important way to engage, but also feels the moral obligation to be too great a burden.

The challenges of care only begin in the office for Alicia. The complexity of the caring relationships in her personal life creates an additional moral burden. Caring for others and maintaining relationships is hard emotional work. It involves being invested in others, identifying with them, and making their interests your own. It is tedious if often rewarding moral labor. Even so, a caring approach to morality isn't supposed to be one-sided. The moral ideal is that in the same way we approach others from a perspective of care, they should do the same for us. That is, sometimes (at the very least) we are supposed to be the ones cared for. The problem arises when this is not the case.

A care ethic also isn't intended to be entirely other directed. The self is also supposed to be among the proper recipients of care. The highest stage of moral development on Gilligan's theory reflects a moral agent who can balance care for herself and care for others. When the practical burdens of caring become too great, however, the moral ideals of care for the self probably slip away. It's no wonder Alicia faces the threat of burnout both emotionally and morally. That Alicia faces the threat of burnout should not be enough to cause us to dismiss the value of a care ethic, but it does make clear that caring needs to be a shared burden. It can't be a strictly one-sided arrangement.

Reconsidering Care

Experiences like Alicia's prompt numerous feminist critiques of a care ethic. One feminist challenge reflects the fact that the values of a care ethic typically develop out of traditional women's labor. It's likely that Alicia has developed a caring approach partly because she has spent much of her life caring for children and a husband. Being a wife and mother is admirable and socially important work, but more tightly connecting women to this sort of labor is not in our best interests.

I value the moral work I do as a mother. It's the most important aspect of my life. I would give up anything else that I thought threatened that moral work. Alicia gives up Will when she thinks her relationship with him has threatened the quality of her mothering. No doubt this decision was painful, but we get the sense that she didn't have to seriously consider the right move. I this way, I suspect Alicia is like most mothers. She makes the relevant sacrifices without a second thought. That women value their work as mothers and caregivers doesn't mean that it should be the basis for moral theory. Women need more freedom to make different choices, not additional moral motivations to be constrained by obligations of care.

This objection can be met by the recognition that a care ethic isn't intended strictly for women. The expectation is that men should also be able to act according to a care ethic. Perhaps in order for that to really occur, men also need more experience at caring labor. If caring were considered a more important moral trait, it might also raise the social value of much of women's labor.

As long as women actually bear the brunt of society's caring labor, women will be profoundly more burdened by the obligation to care. Alicia is expected to care for lots of people. Her children are front and center, along with Peter (even though he doesn't make it easy), her mother-in-law, Will, Kalinda, and even her brother Owen. And that doesn't even include the clients! In these ways, Alicia may be much like many other women struggling to balance numerous obligations including work and family. This probably explains why I am so drawn to her. As a single mother with a full-time faculty position, I identify all too well with Alicia's struggles. I admire her caring approach at the same time that I recognize her bind and her frustration.

Unpaid Labor

Women handle the vast majority of all the caring responsibility in the home, the workplace, and in social institutions. This inequality burdens women with both the moral burden of caring, and also with a distinct economic burden. Much caring labor is unpaid labor; caring for children, parents, and friends carries with it no economic benefit. Time spent at caring is also time not spent at paid labor or moving forward a career.

When women are expected to engage in more caring labor than men in traditional workplaces, women potentially suffer morally, emotionally, and economically. Caring can be a valuable and admirable moral approach—the world needs people like Judge Abernathy and people like Alicia Florrick. Both are appealing moral characters in their own ways—Alicia remains appealing even in the face of feminist criticisms of a care ethic. But so long as society continues to push the caring burden to women, women bearing moral burdens like Saint Alicia will continue to be the norm.

III

The Defense
Rests

6
Are Judges Always Biased?

MARK D. WHITE

As any reader of this book will agree, *The Good Wife* is excellent legal drama. Like all excellent legal drama, it shows idealistic lawyers fighting with opportunistic ones in the courtroom as well as within their own firms. It features heart-wrenching cases, often ripped from the headlines, and always with an element of uncertainty regarding guilt or responsibility that keeps us watching until the end. And it shows how our attractive, svelte lawyers have trouble separating their personal and professional lives.

But let's not forget one essential but oft-overlooked aspect of the legal drama: the judges. Every show has them—sometimes they even share them, as in David E. Kelley's *Ally McBeal* and *The Practice*, both of which took place in Boston (but appeared on different networks). And the more eccentric the better—but this eccentricity does more than add humor and drama to the courtroom proceeding. It also serves to illustrate a persistent issue of debate in legal philosophy: to what degree judges' opinions and biases affect their legal decision-making (or *jurisprudence*).

Formalism Doesn't Just Mean Legal Attire

We like to think that judges are impartial arbiters of the law. The ideal judge, as US Supreme Court Chief Justice John

Roberts is famous for saying, should serve as an "umpire," enforcing rules rather than making them up as he or she goes along. On *The Good Wife*, Judge Park exemplifies this ideal. In all his appearances—particularly in the emotionally charged atmosphere of the hospital in which we often see him—he is formal and fair, guiding trials impartially and apparently without any undue preference for either plaintiff or defendant nor any particular style of argument.

Judge Park's character is consistent with a view of judicial decision-making known as *formalism*, which maintains that legal decisions logically follow from a straightforward application of written law and judicial precedents. If Alicia objects to the prosecution's introduction of evidence that is the result of an illegal search (based on the Fourth Amendment to the US Constitution), then the judge must sustain the objection because the evidence is inadmissible. According to formalists, the law comprises a set of rules that covers every possible legal situation, and the judge exists merely to apply those rules properly to the case at hand. In this sense, the law is like math—or, better yet, chess. Chess consists of rules that both define the game and cover every contingency, leaving little room for ambiguity or discretion on the part of the person overseeing a game. Ideally, there will never be a situation in chess that is not covered by the laws of chess, and there will never be a legal dispute that is not settled by the rules of law.

Not so fast, counselor. While it's a legal fact that evidence obtained through illegal searches is inadmissible, it is not a "fact" that the search was illegal—that's a decision that has to be made by the judge. Even though there are guidelines for what makes a search illegal—mainly in the form of past judicial decisions—they don't clearly determine whether a particular search is illegal, so the judge must decide somehow whether to allow the evidence. This is the fatal flaw of formalism: legal rules, no matter how numerous and detailed, cannot possibly cover every possible situation.

Cases that are easily dealt with according to rules rarely even make it to trial; they are settled or plea-bargained well before they reach a judge. For the rest, the judge must, at some point, make a choice not determined by rules—and that's where the controversy over judicial decision-making begins.

Let's Get Real

Once we acknowledge that judges have to make some decisions that are not settled by rules, we have to figure out how they make them. There are two ways we can look at this: a *descriptive* approach, dealing with how judges actually make decisions, and a *normative* approach, dealing with how they should make decisions. It would seem that the normative approach would be simple: judges should follow the law. But we just saw that it's not always that simple because "the law" doesn't give easy answers to some cases, so judges have to make these decisions using something other than the rules. So there's the question of what they *should* use to fill in the "gaps" in the established law, and the question of what they *actually* do—and there may be different answers to these two questions.

We'll look at normative theories later in this chapter, but for the time being we can stipulate that they involve some moral standards that involve promoting certain ideals for society as a whole. *Legal realism* is an approach to judicial decision-making that claims that judges base their rulings on a wide variety of legal and non-legal factors and not necessarily on any particular normative theory of judicial-making. Legal realists don't argue that judges *shouldn't* make decisions according to any moral standard—they simply argue that in the real world judges *don't*.

Among legal philosophers, legal realism is frequently caricatured and regarded as a joke. It is often said that legal realists maintain that judges make decisions depending on what they had for breakfast or what side of the bed they got up on that morning.

As state's attorney Michael Gladis tells Alicia in "Lifeguard," with respect to sentencing decisions, "a judge has indigestion, you get six months. He has a good meal, someone goes free." In "Double Jeopardy," the military lawyer working with Will and Alicia notes that the judge is "doing another cleanse," implying that she'll be in a bad mood because of it. While no legal realist actually said things as extreme as this, it's reasonable to argue that personality quirks or implicit biases affect judicial decisions in the same way that they affect the decisions made by people like you or me.

None of us is perfectly rational all the time, even if that is the ideal. Our moods, eccentricities, and biases affect our decisions, and other people's decisions are subject to their states of mind when they make them. Certainly, we know when our partners, kids, or bosses are "in the mood" to be told bad news or asked for a favor, and we adjust our behavior accordingly. But legal realists make more substantial claims than this concerning the ways judges make decisions with much more serious ramifications.

Who's the Judge?

Just like the rest of us, lawyers have to adjust their argumentative strategies for the judges they face; as famous lawyer Roy Cohn said, "I don't want to know what the law is, I want to know who the judge is." In *The Good Wife*, like other great legal drama, we often see the attorneys reacting to the news of which judge will be presiding over their classes—and crafting their legal strategies to appeal to him or her. In "Cleaning House" Peter advises Alicia that Judge Hale hates the "fire house defense," but Alicia has to rethink strategy when another judge takes over the case—*and* demands that Alicia wear a skirt in court. In "Fleas," Will encounters Judge Lessner for the first time and quickly learns that she expects to hear "in my opinion" after every argument made. When he stands before her in future episodes, he never fails to say it—thereby gaining her favor—and uses this information to trip up opposing counsel.

Judges have quirks, and good lawyers need to know each judge's unique quirks in order to use them to their advantage, as Will does with Judge Lessner (in his opinion, of course). When facing Judge Abernathy in Season Two's "Wrongful Termination," Will tries to introduce a surprise witness, and when opposing counsel objects, Will "reminds" Abernathy that he likes to err on the side of admitting evidence. (Despite saying he likes to be unpredictable, Abernathy does allow the new witness.) In Season One's "Mock," Will serves as trial judge in a mock court at a local law school as a favor to a friend who teaches there. When student Giada Cabrini asks why he ruled against her motions, he explains that not only was she wrong on the law, but she also lacked humility:

> Life is not the classroom, and judges decide things all the time based on a whim—which attorneys they like, they trust. . . . I said the textbooks go out the window when you're in court. Charm and finesse is [sic] just as important as logic.

Legendary Supreme Court justice Oliver Wendell Holmes, Jr., a key figure in early legal realism, wrote in his landmark 1897 paper "The Path of the Law" that as much as legal scholars go on about "deduction from principles of ethics or admitted axioms or what not," in the end "the prophecies of what the courts will do in fact, and nothing more pretentious, are what I mean by the law."

In Holmes's view, the job of a lawyer is to determine how the judge is going to rule in any particular case, and use that information to the client's best advantage (whether that "client" is a private party or the state). He believed that legal education should support this by focusing on patterns, the ways that certain cases with certain circumstances are often decided and why—regardless of whether those decisions correspond to "principles of ethics or admitted axioms or what not." But individual judges don't necessarily follow these patterns all the time, which highlights the importance to a lawyer of knowing the judge presiding over his or her case.

Prosecutors Are People Too

Personality quirks are one thing, but legal and political biases are another. We expect judges to be human and are willing to excuse them their eccentricities—in my opinion—but we hold them to higher standards of impartiality and objectivity. Everyone has opinions, of course, but we're expected to put them aside when fairness to all is important, such as when someone serves as a judge. That's one reason that Alicia is shocked to discover apparent racial bias in sentencing on the part of Judge Baxter ("Lifeguard") and is no less disgusted when she discovers the disparities were based on kickbacks from a private prison instead.

Good lawyers use knowledge of these biases to serve their clients: in "Nine Hours" Alicia is trying to get a last-minute stay of execution for a death-row inmate. She assesses the judges on the appeals court, and upon discovering that one judge who is regarded as pro-death penalty recently married an anti-death penalty advocate, she focuses her attention on convincing him to grant the appeal (which he does).

Is it reasonable to expect a judge to keep his or her political or moral opinions out of a case? Since judges are in the thick of the legal system and well acquainted with all of the issues and players in it, and the law itself does not provide definite answers to complex cases, how can judges be expected to stay neutral—and what does that even mean? Consider "Silly Season" from Season Two, in which Alicia presents Judge Morris with evidence that the police gave a fake lie-detector test to a suspect—which then "reported" that he was lying—in order to goad him into telling the truth. Obviously disgusted by this, Morris tells the state's attorney, "I know your boss thinks I'm pro-defense. . . . The only problem is when I try to be pro-prosecution, the police pull a stunt like this."

We can presume Judge Morris witnessed many instances of police and prosecutorial misconduct which she regarded as violating the rights of defendants. She may also have seen many cases of shady behavior on the part of defense lawyers, but maybe she feels they're simply doing everything that can—within the law—to combat the resources of the state's attorney's office. The American criminal justice system already grants defendants the presumption of innocence, the right to counsel, and the high "beyond a reasonable doubt" standard of proof. But perhaps Judge Morris feels this is not enough to offset the power of the prosecutor's office, and this leads her to be more sympathetic to objections from the defense attorneys than from the prosecution. Other judges may have the opposite view of the relative status of the prosecution and defense in criminal law and may therefore come to different conclusions when ruling on motions and objections.

Is this bias in the same sense as ruling against a lawyer because of gender, race, or religion? There's certainly no rational basis on which to decide for the prosecution or defense because of personal characteristics of the attorneys or clients in a particular case, but the opinions towards them described in the last paragraph are based on a broader view of the legal system itself.

It seems unreasonable to expect judges to be experts in the law—imperfect as it is—without having some opinions on what's wrong with it and making decisions based on those opinions. So now we'll hear from a philosopher who says that a judge *must* rely on his or her political convictions to decide cases— but only political convictions formed a certain way.

Crossing the Line

Once we start talking about what is right or reasonable for a judge to do, we cross the line from describing what judges actually do to telling them what they *should* do, and we enter the realm of *normative* theories of judicial decision-making. One of the most elaborate and controversial of these theories is offered by legal and political philosopher Ronald Dworkin, and it relates directly to the issue of how a judge should use his or her political convictions when making decisions. But we need to back up a little first, and talk about rules and principles in the law.

H.L.A. Hart, one of the most influential legal philosophers of the twentieth century, wrote in his landmark book *The Concept of Law* that law is best understood as a system of rules. Those rules are legally binding, not only on citizens in their day-to-day lives, but also on judges in their decision-making. But Hart also realized that, as we saw before, the law is not complete. Laws cannot deal with every possible situation because they're written in language, and any language is inherently vague. Hart coined the term *open texture of law* to refer to the "gaps" in the system of rules that makes up the law. While this open texture does leave the law ambiguous—requiring judges to fill it in—it also serves an important purpose, allowing the law a certain flexibility to adapt to changes in society and technology while retaining its core meaning. (Think of the controversies over whether copyright law has to change to adapt to a digital world.)

Hart was very clear on how the system of rules should be structured, but less so when it came to what judges should rely on when making decisions to fill in the gaps in it. He said little more than that judges should have society's best interests at heart when making decisions in the open texture. This led Ronald Dworkin to characterize Hart's view as granting *strong discretion* to judges to make new law to fill in the gaps in existing rules. As Dworkin characterized Hart's view—more generally called *legal positivism*—there is nothing to the law other than rules. When rules don't cover a legal situation, there's nothing else legally binding on judges, thereby freeing them to make whatever decisions they choose to make. In the hands of an ideal, civic-minded judge this may be unproblematic, but if we consider corrupt judges like Judge Baxter from "Lifeguard," we might not be comfortable with vesting so much power in their rulings.

A Matter of Principle

As opposed to Hart's strong discretion, Dworkin argued that judges should have only *weak discretion* when making decisions. According to him, there's more to the law than rules alone, and when all sources of law are included, judges are left with very little leeway in making decisions.

Dworkin emphasizes the role of *principles* in the law, which work differently than rules. Rules are conditional statements in the form of "if x then y": for example, if a search is found to be illegal, then the evidence discovered during the search is inadmissible. A rule either applies or it doesn't, and if two rules conflict, we need another rule to decide which one applies. Principles, on the other hand, are more general, representing ideals of justice or fairness, such as the principles of equality before the law and the rights of free speech and association. Principles both ground and limit the application of rules. Principles like *stare decisis* ("let the decision stand") and legislative deference support rules and enhance the stability of the legal system. When judges overturn rules, however, their decisions are based on principle as well, such as when state-sanctioned racial segregation was declared illegal in the landmark 1954 Supreme Court case *Brown v. Board of Education.*

To use Hart's terminology, Dworkin argues that principles fill in the open texture within and between rules. When a rule's vague, the judge should look for a relevant principle to flesh it out. When two rules conflict, the judge should find the right principle to settle the conflict and choose the more important rule. And when a novel situation arises that no existing rule covers, the judge has to decide what principle applies to the situation. If more than one principle applies in any of these cases, the judge then has to weigh them and determine which one is most important to the decision at hand. Once the correct principle has been found, the judge arrives at the "right answer," the one that is consistent with the legal system containing both rules and principles.

Where do these principles come from? They're usually not written down the way rules are, such as those found in statutes and regulations. They must be read—or, more accurately, *interpreted*—out of judicial opinions, founding documents (such as the Declaration of Independence and the Constitution), and, most generally, the legal and political history of a country. If Dworkin's right, judges are expected to form thorough and elaborate legal-political philosophies, from which they can find principles to decide any legal case not settled by rules—and even some that are, if the rules are found to be unjust when compared to a principle. Not for nothing did Dworkin name his hypothetical judge Hercules!

Even he—Dworkin, not Hercules—knew that this was an insurmountable task, but one that judges nonetheless should aspire to in order to fulfill their duty as judges. (Will would rather like being compared to Hercules, right?)

The Right Answer (Eli's Favorite Concept)

Dworkin presents his theory of judicial decision-making as both normative *and* descriptive, arguing that his theory is not merely how judges should make decisions but also how they actually do make decisions.

What do legal realists think of this? Some of them appreciate that Dworkin expands the concept of law beyond rules to what legal positivists like Hart consider "extra-legal" factors. This fits in with the legal realists' basic argument that legal decisions are usually best explained by nonlegal reasoning. But to the extent that Dworkin regards principles as part of the law and determining the "right answer" to any legal problem, some legal realists consider Dworkin to be a formalist (albeit in a much elaborate way than the early formalists, who thought that written law could answer all legal questions).

One argument against the charge that Dworkin is a closet formalist is that, while he does argue that principles will lead a judge to the "right answer," each judge will arrive at his or her unique philosophy of the legal system and set of principles derived from it. When Dworkin writes of the right answer, he doesn't mean "right" as in 4 is the right answer to 2 + 2. (We'd better have Kalinda fact-check that.) He means that it's the right answer in terms of that judge's philosophy, the one that maintains the integrity of the legal system as he or she sees it. For this reason, Dworkin's jurisprudence is often called the "integrity theory of the law."

If we can imagine Judges Abernathy and Lessner both presiding over the same case, each would arrive at his or her "right answer," which may be different decisions, or the same decision made for different reasons. Even if they recognized the same principles relevant to the cases, they may find different ones to be most important, resulting in different decisions. This is definitely not formalism as we discussed it earlier: even if decisions do flow from the principles a judge picks out, the principles themselves are part of the judge's decision-making process. Chess players don't pick their rules because that's how they feel the game is played—but to some extent, judges do in Dworkin's system.

We can now return to the issue of judges and their political opinions. We said above that Dworkin requires each judge to form an exhaustive philosophy of the legal-political system in order to make decisions. For instance, in reference to the United States, some judges will study its history, laws, and foundational documents and interpret them as being grounded in liberty and rights. Others will do the same exhaustive study but interpret into the history a focus on welfare and equality. And others will come up with yet more interpretations. Each judge's interpretation leads to a unique legal-political philosophy that informs his or her decision— and *this* is the sense in which judges' political views enter their decisions, through their underlying philosophy of how the legal system in this country (or any other country) works.

Dworkin's distinction is a fine one, to be sure: judges can, indeed must, rely on their dispassionate philosophical interpretation of the legal and political systems, but should avoid their more personal political positions. Of course, in many cases these will coincide—a judge like Abernathy has liberal personal positions and is also known to rule on the liberal side. In "Wrongful Termination," Alicia tells Stern (whom she's opposing):

> It's Judge Abernathy. You're representing a deep-pocketed big, bad, internet company who treated its employees so poorly, three of them committed suicide in a month—this one in his own cubicle. What side do *you* think Abernathy will be on?

This kind of convergence of personal political beliefs and abstract political philosophy explains why judges—especially Supreme Court justices—are often characterized as liberal or conservative in their personal politics rather than their deeper legal philosophy.

But this is not necessarily always the case. For instance, Supreme Court Justice Anthony Kennedy, a devout Catholic, voted in 1992's *Planned Parenthood v. Casey* to support and refine the pro-choice result of 1973's *Roe v. Wade*. Even though he personally opposed abortion, he explained that he felt *Roe v. Wade* was the established law of the land, part of the history and tradition of the country, which he should not overturn out of mere personal conviction. If judges focus on maintaining the integrity of the legal system—as Justice Kennedy did in *Casey*—they can avoid injecting their personal political and moral beliefs into their decisions. They should always strive to be impartial, but this has to be understood *within* their interpretations of the law.

Will's So Smart

Judges are human like the rest of us, and they work within a legal system developed by humans over centuries of different cultures and governments. As a result, they are not—and they cannot be—the perfectly rational and impartial "umpires" we might like them to be.

The legal realists teach us that sometimes judges base their decisions on more than "just" legal rules, for better or for worse, and Dworkin offers one example of what should ground those decisions. No legal philosopher would argue that judges should make decisions and rulings based on legally irrelevant factors like the lawyers' race or gender, though they disagree on what the legally relevant factors are.

But one thing is clear: when rules don't tell them the answer, judges have to use something else, and lawyers—for the good of their clients—do well to recognize this and try to predict what it is. As Will tells Ms. Cabrini in "Mock," "to succeed in court, you need to work on everything"—and that goes for judges too.

7
Why Should I Believe You?

LISA MCNULTY

Alicia Florrick has faced the betrayal of her husband, followed by the public humiliation of having the story of that betrayal depicted on television on twenty-four-hour rotation. Many of the people she thought of as friends have abandoned her. She is re-entering a profession where she's likely to face lies and deceit. We often see uppermost in Alicia's concerns questions about trust: Who can I trust now? Who should I believe?

Good Evidence

One straightforward answer to this question might be *'Because there is good evidence that I am telling the truth'*. Often it is Alicia herself who uncovers such evidence on behalf of her clients, and there's something particularly satisfying about placing some conclusive piece of evidence before the court, which overrides earlier suppositions.

If Brian O'Neill was where he claimed to be when the security guard died, the sprinklers would have soaked him; the sprinklers did not soak him, therefore, he was not there ("Home"). The security tape shows a plastic bag floating in the breeze at precisely 11:48 P.M. three nights in a row, therefore the tape must have been duplicated. ("Pilot"). When Alicia has gathered strong, independent evidence supporting what her client says, she of course has excellent reason to believe that they're telling the truth. Furthermore, she is in a good position to convincingly support and argue it to others; namely a judge and jury.

But there is another way to answer the question *'Why should I believe you?'* It is possible to respond not in a strictly evidence-based way but in a moral way: *'Because I deserve to be believed by you. I have that right'*. This response can arise for several reasons. It could be that this person is a friend, or a member of one's family. It could be that you have a special kind of personal responsibility for this person, as Alicia experiences with her clients. Or it could simply be that your disbelief of this person will lead to them being hurt in some way. This could easily happen if you are a judge or a member of a jury, as a person's freedom may hang in the balance. But even as a stranger, your disbelief could hurt someone, especially if you pass your opinion on to others.

So, can someone deserve to be believed, even when no strong evidence can be produced in their favor, or perhaps even when the available evidence seems to be against them? Is there such a thing as a right to be believed, or a right to be believed by certain people? Is there a corresponding moral duty to believe certain people? And, if so, what exactly does this duty demand from us? There are tough questions here.

A Duty to Believe?

We can begin by considering what our moral duty is in general, and how we can discover it. Immanuel Kant proposes the Categorical Imperative as a means to discover whether actions are morally acceptable. According to the Categorical Imperative, you should: *Act only according to that maxim whereby you can, at the same time, will that it should become a universal law.*

Every action we perform has an underlying maxim. For example, when Peter lies to Alicia, his action has the underlying maxim 'It's okay to lie'. In order to discover whether his action, lying, is in accordance with his moral duty, Peter could have run his action through the Categorical Imperative, imagining a world in which this maxim was a universal law: everyone habitually tells lies. This produces a kind of contradiction. Telling a lie is saying something untrue, with the intention of someone believing that it is true. Telling a lie requires that someone trusts you. Yet in a world where everyone told lies whenever they wanted to, people would not trust one another, and so it would become impossible to lie successfully.

When Peter lies, he's making a sort of mistake. He's treating himself as exceptional, as though it's permissible for him to act in this way, but not for people in general to act in the same way. But he's not exceptional. Like every other human being, he is answerable to his duty, in this case the duty to tell the truth.

It's not immediately obvious, however, whether we would have a duty to *believe* people. It seems equally unwise to *always* follow the maxim 'I shall believe what is told to me', and the maxim 'I shall not believe what is told to me'. If we doubt people universally, then we will make little progress in life, whilst if we believe people universally, then we shall have many untrue beliefs. The most plausible alternative would be the maxim 'I shall proportion my belief to the evidence'. But this would imply that if it would be reasonable for a stranger with all the relevant information to disbelieve your friend, then you should disbelieve them too.

The difficulty is that Kant regards our moral duty as something in contrast to, and often in conflict with, our desire to do things out of emotional concern for others. This would include our biases towards friends and family, and others we feel particularly responsible for. If I believe someone because I am emotionally moved to do so, I may be acting against my Kantian duty: or at any rate, there is little sense in which I could have a moral obligation to believe someone because of such a connection.

So, is the fact that someone is your friend in itself a good reason to believe them? Certainly not in the sense that you want some guarantee that your beliefs must be true. The fact that a person happens to be Alicia's husband, or son, or friend, does not in itself mean that they are automatically telling her the truth or should be one hundred percent trusted without some vetting or established sense of trust.

Peter, her husband, obviously betrayed his wife very deeply; Zach, her son, hides packages of photographs from her; Kalinda, her colleague and friend, has a very bad record indeed when it comes to deceit and secrets. So, the fact of a personal relationship does not in itself give what philosophers call good *epistemic* reasons to believe the person. It also does not necessarily make them reliable.

However, when we choose to believe a friend, we are certainly *not* exactly assessing their trustworthiness, in order to mentally calculate the likelihood of them telling the truth or a lie on this or that occasion. Anyone with a reasonable amount of information about them could do that, and to do so would be to treat this person as *evidence to be assessed*, rather than as a *friend to be trusted*.

A stranger might assess your friend's evidence and find it wanting. Believing someone because they are your friend means not subjecting them to the same level of assessment as a stranger reasonably might. We see Alicia granting this privilege to her friends. Consider the example of Kenny Chatham ("You Can't Go Home Again"). Accused of murder, he calls upon Alicia to act as his lawyer. She's aware that he has previously committed a crime, albeit a minor one of taking illegal drugs. Kenny's parents have themselves selected a lawyer on behalf of their son, one with more experience than Alicia. Yet Kenny chooses Alicia because she's a friend, who will genuinely be on his side.

Alicia chooses to continue as Kenny's lawyer, because she cares a great deal more about Kenny than his parents' lawyer does. She believes him, and there's a definite moral element to this belief: she believes *in* the little boy that she saw grow up, which makes it very natural for her to believe that he is telling the truth, and to defend him. Fortune smiles on Alicia here; she turns out to be correct in her belief that Kenny is innocent, and able to prove her case. But this is something that she discovers after her determination to defend him, not something that prompts it in the first place.

Belief and Betrayal

So is Alicia acting in accordance with her duty? She certainly ends by proportioning her belief to the evidence. But she does not begin this way; she begins by trusting Kenny's word. It is perhaps not an attitude she would have taken towards Kenny had she not had a personal connection. But there's a caveat. Alicia is more ready to believe Kenny than a stranger would be, because he has earned her trust through past behaviour. Perhaps it's true that if a stranger with all the relevant information would disbelieve Kenny, then so should Alicia. But a stranger would not have access to the same information that Alicia does, precisely because she would lack that personal connection.

Perhaps there's something in the idea that we should readily believe people whom we are personally committed or connected to. Our friends can reasonably expect us to be more ready to believe them than we would a stranger in the same circumstances. Arguably this is a key sign of friendship. But it would be a mistake to regard this as an unquestionable and permanent state of affairs. Kenny's privilege was earned, and could be lost again. We don't believe our friends *in all circumstances*, even when there's overwhelming evidence against what they are saying.

Alicia presumably believed her husband to be faithful; but having been faced with overwhelming evidence to the contrary, she can't be expected to continue to believe this now. We trust our friends because they have earned our trust, and they can always lose it again. So, our friends have special privileges only because they have earned them. Can we then, have any obligation to believe a stranger, when evidence is absent or even goes against them?

The most familiar and simplest example of this in Alicia's experience is the principle that defendants in a courtroom are 'innocent until proven guilty'. 'Proof' here is taken to be evidence *beyond reasonable doubt*. The greater burden of proof lies with the prosecution, since it is their job to demonstrate the guilt of the defendant. This is not because the accused has been evaluated in any way and found to be more likely innocent than guilty before the trial has even begun. It's a moral consideration. If the court disbelieves the defense, and finds the accused guilty, then the court will punish the accused. In some places certain crimes are punishable by death: a legal process known as capital punishment where the jury's guilty verdict will result in the execution of the individual on trial. The greater our power, the greater the need for certainty. As Alicia says, "So much of what we do is uncertain. To do this to a man . . . It has to be right" ("Nine Hours").

The power of the judge and jury produces in them an obligation, a duty to believe the defendant until she is proven guilty. But there are other positions of power we may hold in relation to a speaker wishing to be believed. The kind of power we have, and the extent of that power, may affect the obligations we have. The Season Three episode "The Death Zone" illustrates this complication well.

Danny Lambrose has written a book, entitled *My Brother's Peak*, which describes his brother's final ascent of Everest and his death on that climb. In this book, he claims that another mountaineer, named Oliver Cardiff, "not only stepped over Robert's body to get to the summit but then took his bottled oxygen," thereby abandoning Robert to die. Cardiff vehemently denies this, and brings a suit against Lambrose for libel. When the suit fails, he begins another, this time under English law. It is generally much, much easier to convict someone of libel under English law than under American law.

Who Has the Right to Be Believed?

To answer this question, we must consider what our position of power is. Imagine that you were an ordinary reader of Lambrose's book. It's likely that you would engage with the author's perspective, sympathize with him, and would (if you allowed yourself to do so) become very much prejudiced against Oliver Cardiff, and assume that he's guilty. Whilst you know that Cardiff denies the actions Lambrose accuses him of, you may be inclined to believe Lambrose over Cardiff. *Should* you?

If you become convinced that Cardiff is guilty of abandoning a man to die, then you have already contributed to the destruction of Cardiff's reputation; which, after all, is nothing but the sum of personal opinions. If you go on to express that belief to others, then you will increase still further the public perception that he is little better than a murderer. You don't have the power of a judge or jury, but the power you do have also comes with responsibility. It seems plausible to say that, to be just to Cardiff, you should be certain beyond reasonable doubt that he abandoned a man to die, before you allow yourself to believe it; and certainly before you spread rumors about him. It is doubtful, to say the least, that Lambrose's book could provide you with such powerful evidence.

Unfortunately, your alternative is not ideal; since you have power over Lambrose's reputation, too. You would have to believe that the book contains untruths, which is a slur on Lambrose's character; you would be presuming that Lambrose failed to meet a moral duty you expect of yourself (i.e., giving Cardiff the benefit of the doubt). However, in the circumstances, this is a comparatively minor slur, especially if you choose to regard him as a mourning relative mistaken about the strength of the evidence, rather than as a liar.

On balance, as a reader of *My Brother's Peak*, you have a greater power over Cardiff than you do over Lambrose. This power gives you a responsibility to assume that Cardiff did not abandon Robert to die, until you have overwhelming evidence to suggest that he did; and in particular, to refrain from damaging Cardiff's reputation further by word of mouth, until you encounter such evidence.

Now consider the position of the judge in the first trial against Lambrose. This position of power is very different to that of a reader of Lambrose's book, and much more straightforward. If you believe that Cardiff (or rather Cardiff's lawyer) is telling the truth, then you must convict Lambrose for libel.

This power gives you a responsibility: to regard Lambrose as innocent of libel, until you have overwhelming evidence to suggest that he is guilty; and not to convict him unless you encounter such evidence during the course of the trial.

Belief and Harm

Is this a good reason to believe someone? There is a sense in which this is obviously wrong. Your power over someone's reputation, or over whether or not they are found guilty of a crime, does not in itself have any impact on whether or not that person's telling the truth. But there is another sense in which your power gives you a duty; an obligation to *assume* truthfulness, until proven otherwise. Kant would perhaps agree that this is our duty, since we could not rationally will the existence of a world in which reputations were carelessly destroyed.

The case of "The Death Zone" seems to show that if we do have such an obligation, what we ought to believe changes with *what our position of power* is. Read the book, and you are obliged to believe Cardiff. But suppose that the judge on the libel case happened to have read the book beforehand. The moment he steps into the courtroom, his position of power changes from that of a reader to that of a judge. So too his obligation changes: he is now obliged to believe Lambrose (until such a time as he is proven guilty).

Perhaps, then, there are times when we have a duty to believe someone not especially because of the convincingness of their evidence but because of our position in relation to that person: a personal relationship, or a position of power. The latter opens a strange possibility: should our position of power change, our obligations could suddenly reverse. This is a puzzling idea. Can this sort of cognitive flexibility really be expected of us? Can we actually do this? Even if we can, *ought* we?

Pascal's Wager

Can we choose what to believe? This is a key issue for Pascal's Wager. Pascal's argument does not seek to prove the existence of God, but rather, to persuade people that they should choose to believe in God. Effectively, we're 'betting' on God's existence, or his non-existence; and when we make a bet, it is best to assess the dangers and benefits of betting each way.

First, suppose that you believe in God, and it turns out that God doesn't exist. Admittedly, your hopes of Heaven have been thwarted, but then you aren't around to be disappointed by this fact. So what have you lost? Some wasted hours in church perhaps (depending on whether you actually enjoyed being there), some opportunities for enjoyable sins. But, you have lost nothing that prevented you from having a generally pleasant life.

Secondly, suppose that you don't believe in God, and it turns out that God does exist. The cost seems much higher. Not only do you not go to Heaven, but also you spend eternity in Hell. You have, admittedly, been able to sleep in every Sunday and, if you were so inclined, to get involved with various activities of which God may not approve. But on balance, you have things worse as a mistaken atheist than would as a mistaken theist.

Imagine that Pascal has convinced you that believing in God would be a good idea. Yet, currently, you do not believe in God. What can you do next? Having decided that it would be for the best that you believe something, there is still a further thing to achieve: you *actually changing my belief*, choosing one belief over another as an act of will. But that degree of self-control would be unusual to say the least. You can't simply flip a switch in your head from 'un-believer' to 'believer'. So what exactly are you supposed to *do*?

Behaving Like a Believer

Pascal is aware of this problem. His response is that if we want to believe in God, we should act as though we believed in God already. Behaving like a believer might include such things as reading the Bible, attending church, and taking communion. Gradually, these habits of action affect our habits of thinking. Behaving like a believer provides us with the best possible chance of becoming one.

Whilst Pascal is focusing on our belief in God, we might use a similar method in order to believe other people. Suppose that I become convinced that I have a moral obligation to believe someone. However, at the moment, I simply don't believe them. What can I do about it? What would behaving like a believer mean here?

Suppose that the reader of Lambrose's book agrees that her influence on Cardiff's reputation gives her an obligation to believe Cardiff (until any point when the evidence against him becomes overwhelming). What exactly is she obliged to do? Certainly not to immediately and straightforwardly change her existing belief. It seems unlikely that this is something that she *can* do. But perhaps we can say that she is obliged to *behave as though she believed* that Cardiff did not leave a man to die. *Behaving as though she believed* means refraining from using the power she has against him: essentially, *not* spreading rumors to further damage his reputation.

So far, this seems reasonable. However, in Pascal's recommendation, *behaving like a believer* is not the end of the story. It's a means to an end: a form of self-manipulation. You have been fully successful only when you *actually have the belief.* Would behaving like a believer actually make the reader believe? It's possible, but by no means is it necessary. She may well remain personally convinced that Lambrose is right, that Cardiff is guilty; even whilst acknowledging that neither Lambrose not she can prove it beyond reasonable doubt. Provided that she acknowledges this, and provided that she does not suggest to others that there is good reason to think of Cardiff is guilty, then she has surely done nothing wrong.

Furthermore, we may wish to say that she has a duty *not* to manipulate her beliefs in the Pascalian way, even if she could. This is because the more adept she becomes at such self-manipulation, the less likely she would be to reassess her belief even in the light of overwhelming evidence. Suppose evidence reaches her attention that makes it overwhelmingly likely that Cardiff did take the oxygen and abandon a man to die. It may plausibly become, if not her moral duty, then at least a praiseworthy action to draw the attention of the world to this, so that neither Cardiff nor another similarly irresponsible climber will dare to act in this way again. Thinking of this in terms of the Categorical Imperative, we can say that the maxim 'It is acceptable to manipulate one's own beliefs' is not one which we would wish to see universalized.

Similarly, the judge is obliged to *behave as though he believed* that Lambrose is innocent of libel, until proven guilty. This behavior is reflected in not giving a 'guilty' verdict unless there is evidence beyond reasonable doubt that he is guilty of libel. Yet behaving as though he believed would not necessarily make him believe. It is possible that in a circumstance where there is insufficient evidence to convict a defendant, the judge may nonetheless be personally convinced of the defendant's guilt. Curiously, Scottish law reflects this by allowing three possible verdicts: 'guilty', 'not guilty', and 'not proven'. The last is commonly understood to mean 'not guilty, but don't do it again'; and is perhaps a means by which the judge's full beliefs on the matter might be expressed.

Behaving Like a Good Wife

> I spent fifteen years . . . never asking a single question, because I didn't think I had to. And he took everything I thought we had and he just put it out there for everyone.
>
> — ALICIA, in "Pilot," Season One

Peter's betrayal of Alicia destroyed her trust. Yet whilst Alicia no longer believes in her marriage, she does behave like a believer. Sometimes, this is simply to shape the perceptions of others: publicly holding her husband's hand; taking him back into her home when he was released under electronic monitoring. But there are clearly times when Alicia is behaving like a believer with the goal of actually changing her beliefs; of coming again to believe her husband and believe in her marriage. When Alicia runs away from her kiss with Will to have sex with Peter, she is trying to convince herself that she still has a marriage. She is Pascal's atheist, taking communion.

With the benefit of hindsight, we may simply wish to say that it didn't work, that her marriage was past saving. Yet Alicia has a deep emotional investment here. She stands a better chance than either the reader or the judge of Pascal's method actually working; of ending up by believing again. And certainly, unless she comes to believe in her marriage again, it *is* over. Possibly, this is her best shot as saving the marriage.

If Alicia can come to believe in her marriage again in this way, ought she to do so? This is a difficult question. The choice to continue with her marriage or to end it lies with her, and whether or not we judge that her marriage isn't worth saving matters little. What matters more is that, if she were successful in the Pascalian method, then she would not have the necessary distance to evaluate whether *she* thought her marriage was worth saving or not.

Does Peter have a privilege, a moral right to be believed by his wife? Maybe once he did. Alicia spending fifteen years *not* constantly expecting infidelity was an entirely appropriate thing to do. But that privilege granted him a lesser burden of proof, not the right to be believed against all the available evidence.

Peter's betrayal has destroyed any privilege he may once have had. It has broken the spell. A friend does have a privilege, a moral right to our trust and belief, but that privilege was originally gained through evidence that this person was worthy of trust and friendship. This privilege can be and has been lost. Peter had no moral right either to Alicia's belief, or to her behaving like a believer in public or in private. As far as believing goes, Alicia has no moral obligation to behave like a good wife.

8
Doing the Wrong Thing for a Good Reason

JAMES EDWIN MAHON

The Good Wife is great TV in part because it depicts bad people doing what's morally wrong, and good people doing what's morally right. The good people doing what's right are usually the litigators at the white-shoe Chicago law firm of Lockhart Gardner, and the bad people doing what's wrong are usually the deep-pocketed businesses they are suing on behalf of their clients.

In the Season One episode, "Crash," the bad people are Crossnational Freight, a train company. They knew from a previous near-collision that their freight trains had faulty pressure sensors, and that their trains were running at higher speeds than their drivers believed. When one of these trains crashes, killing the three drivers, they try to blame the crash on the drivers, claiming that they were driving too fast. By blaming the crash on the drivers they can avoid paying the drivers' widows their pensions. Indeed, Crossnational Freight's unscrupulous lawyer, Patti Nyholm, who knows that the trains had faulty sensors, wants to counter-sue the dead drivers and their widows for the cost of the train.

As Linda, one of the three widows, says to Lockhart Gardner attorney Alicia Florrick at the trackside memorial to her husband and the other two dead drivers, "For the longest time, I didn't think there was evil. I just thought there were people, who did good and bad things. But now . . ." In the end, a sympathetic Crossnational Freight employee blows the whistle on the train company (no play on words intended). With Alicia's help, the widows get a large payout, as well as an official apology from the company.

If the show only depicted bad people doing what's morally wrong, and good people doing what's morally right, then it would not be as good a TV show as it is. For *The Good Wife* also depicts *bad* people doing what is *morally right*. Or at least, it depicts wholly self-interested people doing what is morally right. In the Season Two episode, "In Sickness," the same unscrupulous lawyer, Patti Nyholm, is defending Harbor Hospital. The hospital has taken one of their patients, Marjorie Garnett, off the liver transplant waiting list just as a new liver has become available. Will Gardner, along with Alicia, has brought an emergency injunction against Harbor Hospital on behalf of Marjorie.

In the middle of the trial, Patti is fired by her law firm and given a paltry liquidation of contract payment. In an effort to get her firm to pay out a lot more, or to hire her back, Patti immediately sues for wrongful termination and hires Lockhart Gardner as her counsel. She now assists Will and Alicia in their case against the hospital and her former firm.

Patti tells a fairy tale to her baby about a hospital that charges patients for expensive unnecessary tests, with the baby monitor turned on (intentionally), and this fairy tale is 'overheard' by Will and Alicia in another room. It enables them to discover that one of the hospital's doctors is ordering excessive CT scans of patients whom he deems to be unsuitable recipients of donor livers. As a result of Patti's help, Lockhart Gardner is able to get Marjorie the donated liver and start a class action suit against Harbor Hospital on behalf of other patients who have been over-tested. The firm must bring the suit, however, without Patti's help, since she has been re-hired by her law firm to represent the hospital and fight the suit.

Patti never experiences a change of heart. She never stops being motivated by self-interest at the expense of other people's well being. She helps the liver patient's lawyers against the hospital solely in order to get leverage over her firm, and she stops as soon as the maneuver works and she's hired back by her firm. Nevertheless, her short-lived assisting of Will and Alicia helps save a life. The ethical complexity of her behavior is that she does what is morally right—she helps Will and Alicia save Marjorie's life—from a motive that is entirely calculating and self-interested.

Doing the Right Thing for the Wrong Reason

It's not just other attorneys who do what's morally right from bad motives (or at least, from naked self-interest). The attorneys of Lockhart Gardner also do what is morally right from less than admirable motives. Indeed, Alicia herself does what is morally right because it's expedient. The difference is that she struggles with the ethical conflict.

In "Great Firewall," the law firm is suing Neil Gross, the CEO of social networking site Chumhum, on behalf of a Chinese dissident blogger, Shen Yuan. Chumhum handed over Shen Yuan's secret IP address to the Chinese authorities, and as a result Shen Yuan spent five years in a Chinese prison, being tortured for several of those years. Stern, Lockhart, and Gardner's bottom-line demand in their suit is that Chumhum stop handing over the IP addresses of political dissidents to the Chinese authorities. They do not reveal it at first, even to Alicia, but their reason for taking on this case is that they want Chumhum to get out of China so that their other client, billionaire social network site creator Patric Edelstein, can set up his own networking site in China.

When Alicia discovers the real reason they're suing Chumhum, she confronts Will Gardner. Will defends the firm's action.

> It's a good case, no matter what. Shen Yuan was tortured, imprisoned.

Yes. But that's not why we're pursuing it.

Alicia—

I just for one minute wanted to think that we were doing the right thing.

But we are doing the right thing.

But for the wrong reason.

Who do you know is doing something for the right reason? I would love to meet them, because my guess is, after five minutes of questioning, we'll find the wrong reason.

You believe that?

I do believe that. And if you thought about all you've learned this past year, you'd believe it too.

Insofar as Alicia has seen Patti Nyholm doing the morally "right thing"—helping Marjorie Garnett get a donated liver—for the "wrong reason"—from self-interest—Will is correct that Alicia does know of people who have done what is morally right from the motive of self-interest. Indeed, given that Lockhart Gardner received a large payout from the class action suit on behalf of all of the patients of Harbor Hospital who were over-tested, Will may be right that most or all lawsuits are motivated by self-interest. Nevertheless, Alicia feels conflicted about suing Chumhum in order to benefit their other client. She feels conflicted about doing what's morally right from the motive of self-interest.

Doing the Wrong Thing for the Right Reason

The Good Wife also depicts *good* people doing what is *morally wrong*. In the first season episode, "Fixed," a husband and wife team, Ray and Carol Demory, are suing Zenapril Pharmaceutical for damages. Zenapril manufactures a migraine drug that caused Ray to have a brainstem stroke that put him in a wheelchair for life. The Demorys are a test case for a class action lawsuit involving 138 victims that Lockhart Gardner is bringing against Zenapril.

Zenapril claims that the drug was never supposed to be used for migraines, but in court Diane Lockhart shows that they applied to market Zenapril as a migraine drug in Europe. In order to be sure of a victory that will help all of the victims of the drug, however, the Demorys bribe the jury foreman. By the time Alicia discovers what they've done, the jury has voted to award damages to the Demorys, and the class action lawsuit on behalf of all of the other victims has begun.

"You didn't have to do it. You would have won," she tells Carol Demory. Carol doesn't contradict the charge of bribing the juror. Instead she replies, "We did win." Alicia goes to Diane Lockhart and tells her that they must go to the judge immediately and tell him that their clients bribed a juror. Diane tells her that when they raised their suspicion of jury tampering with the judge earlier in the trial, the judge overruled them. So they have fulfilled their obligations under the law. Meanwhile, as she tells Alicia, "Today you helped a lot of people in pain find justice."

The Demorys are motivated by a desire to help a lot of people who are suffering. They are not motivated merely by self-interest. They carry with them a box containing the photos of the other victims of Zenapril, and constantly seek to comfort the other victims who attend the trial. It's just that, unbeknownst to their lawyers, they decided to bribe someone, in order to help everyone. Although Carol has bought off a juror, and will benefit from the award, she is motivated by altruism. She does what is morally wrong—from a motive that is entirely selfless and loving.

Alicia herself does what is morally wrong from the motive of compassion. In the "Great Firewall" episode, Chumhum's lawyers get an official from the Bush Administration to testify that waterboarding, being made to stand for days, and various other things that were done to Shen Yuan were considered "aggressive interrogation techniques" by the US government from 2004 to 2008, and did not rise to the level of torture. Hence, Shen Yuan cannot claim that he was tortured as a result of Chumhum giving the Chinese authorities his secret IP address. Will and Diane want Alicia to get Shen Yuan to lie and say that he continued to be treated in this way into 2009, when, under the new Obama Administration's definition of 'torture,' he was being tortured according to the US government's definition.

"So you're up for it?" Will asks Alicia. "Convincing him to lie?" Alicia asks. She seems to be hesitant. Diane asks her, "Do you want us to put somebody else on it?" "No," Alicia replies. Off-screen, she convinces Shen Yuan to lie. As a result, although they refuse to pay out any money, Chumhum decides to withdraw from China and vows to never again hand over the IP addresses of users of the social network site to the Chinese authorities. The coast is now clear for the firm's other client to move in on China. Here, it seems, just like the Demorys, Alicia is doing the morally wrong thing for the "right reason."

Alicia herself states on other occasions that it is wrong to lie. When talking to her children, in "In Sickness," about separating from her husband, former State's Attorney Peter Florrick, she tells them that they are to keep this information to themselves. "We don't lie here. We don't lie to each other. But when people want to hurt us, it is sometimes all right to . . . to not tell the full truth." Not telling the full truth is not the same as lying. If lying is morally wrong, then convincing someone to lie is also morally wrong. Nevertheless, Alicia convinces Shen Yuan to lie in order to get Chumhum to stop turning over information about political dissidents to the Chinese authorities.

Her hesitation in agreeing to do this is evidence that she feels conflicted about getting Shen Yuan to lie, even though she wants to prevent more people from being tortured. She experiences a conflict about doing what's morally wrong from the noble motive of compassion for current and future victims of torture and imprisonment.

Reasons and Motives

Will Gardner talks about doing the right thing for the wrong reason. This sounds good, but it's a mistake. A *reason* cannot be right or wrong. 'Right' and 'wrong' are terms that apply to *actions* and not to reasons. A morally right action may be performed for any number of reasons, and a morally wrong action may be performed for any number of reasons. But the reason for performing a right action, or the reason for performing a wrong action, is not right or wrong.

Protecting political dissidents from torture and imprisonment by the Chinese authorities is the right action. But it would be a mistake to say that protecting political dissidents out of compassion is protecting them for the 'right' reason, whereas protecting political dissidents out of self-interest is protecting them from the 'wrong' reason. Reasons just are not the sorts of things that are right or wrong.

A reason is a motive. One does not say of a motive, like jealousy, or fear, or love, or self-interest, or sympathy, or love of humankind, or hatred of humankind, that it is 'right' or 'wrong'. The correct thing to say about motives is that they are good or bad, praiseworthy or blameworthy, admirable or contemptible.

Motives are also a part of morality; they are subject to moral evaluation. The moral evaluation of an action's motive is distinct from the moral evaluation of the action itself. The rightness or wrongness of the action is distinct from the goodness or badness, the praiseworthiness or blameworthiness, of the motive behind the action. A morally good motive for performing a wrong action does not change the fact that the action is wrong. And a morally bad motive for performing a right action does not change the fact that the motive is bad. This is the kernel of truth behind the expression 'doing the right thing for the wrong reason', which should really be 'doing the right thing for a bad reason' or 'doing the right thing from a bad motive'.

Intentions versus Motives

The distinction between actions and motives is essentially the same as the distinction between intentions and motives. In the first edition of *Utilitarianism* in 1861, John Stuart

Mill distinguished between actions and motives. The motive behind an action, he argued, had nothing to do with the moral rightness or the moral wrongness of the action. If a man saves another man from drowning, then he does what is right, whether he is motivated by a sense of duty or by a desire to gain a reward.

In correspondence with Mill, the Reverend J. Llewellyn Davies objected that the moral rightness or the moral wrongness of an action *does* depend upon the motive behind the action. If a tyrant saves an enemy from drowning in order to torture and kill him, then the tyrant does *not* do what is right.

In the second edition of *Utilitarianism* in 1863, Mill added a footnote in which he discussed Davies's objection. He replied that Davies had confused *motive* with *intention*. The tyrant does not 'save' an enemy from the motive of a desire to torture and kill him. Rather, the tyrant has an *intention* to torture and kill his enemy. This is why he pulls the enemy out of the water.

The moral wrongness of what the tyrant does depends entirely on his intention. However, the motive, that is, the feeling that makes the tyrant form the intention to torture and kill, if it makes no difference to the action, makes no difference to the wrongness of the action. The intent to torture and kill someone is not a *motive*. If a tyrant intends to torture and kill an enemy, then he may be motivated to do this by a sadistic desire or by a desire to win a bet. His action is wrong, however, regardless of whether he is motivated by a sadistic desire or a desire to win a bet.

Mill's point is that intending to save a life is morally right, regardless of the motive behind the intention to save a life (a sense of duty, a feeling of benevolence, a desire for a reward) However, he does add that our moral estimation of the person will differ, depending on his motive. We have a *higher* moral estimation of the person who saves a life from the motive of a sense of duty or from the motive of benevolence than of the person who saves a life in order to gain a reward, even if, in each case, the person does what is morally right.

What's important about Mill's distinction between intention and motive, and his consequent distinction between more and less morally estimable motives, is that it does not depend in any way upon his particular account of moral rightness. The distinction is entirely independent of utilitarianism, which holds that an action is morally right as it tends to promote happiness, and morally wrong as it tends to promote unhappiness. An entirely different account of the moral rightness of actions can preserve Mill's distinction.

In the *Groundwork for the Metaphysics of Morals* in 1785, Immanuel Kant provides an example of a person doing what is morally right from the motive of self-interest. A shopkeeper, he says, can charge every customer the same price, in order to earn a reputation for fair dealing, and as a result make a profit. The shopkeeper does what's morally right in charging every customer the same price. Indeed, he does what is morally obligatory, Kant would say. However, he does not do this because it is the morally right thing to do. His motive for doing this is not the motive of duty. His motive is self-interest.

For Kant, an action is morally right if and only if everyone is treated equally. In particular, a person who does what is morally right cannot make an exception for herself, or for others. That would mean applying a double standard. A shopkeeper may not charge different prices to different customers.

Kant's criticism of the shopkeeper who charges every customer the same price in order to make a profit has nothing to do with the shopkeeper's action. The shopkeeper does what is morally right, and his action has what Kant calls *legality*. His criticism is that the shopkeeper lacks a praiseworthy motive, because he acts on the basis of self-interest. A different shopkeeper, who charged every customer the same price from the motive of respect for the customer's equal dignity as a rational person, would be acting from the motive of duty. This is the *only* moral motive for Kant, and it deserves the highest form of praise, which is esteem. In this case, the shopkeeper does what is morally right, and his action has what Kant calls *morality*. Very few shopkeepers have this motive, in Kant's opinion. Possible exceptions include those who work for co-op food markets in Brooklyn, and those who sell vinyl LPs and audiocassette tapes in used music stores in Greenwich Village.

Despite Kant's completely different account of moral rightness, therefore, he accepts the Millian distinction between actions (intentions) and motives, and the consequent distinction between more and less morally estimable motives

Neither Mill nor Kant is interested in defending morally wrong actions that are performed from good motives. Such actions are immoral, they hold, and cannot be justified, regardless of the goodness of the motives behind them. Famously, Kant wrote an essay in 1797, entitled "On a Supposed Right to Lie from Philanthropy," in which he attacked lying from the motive of "philanthropy," or love of fellow man. No motive, according to Kant, can justify doing what is morally wrong.

Doing the Wrong Thing from a Good Motive

Will Gardner is correct that we can do the morally right thing from the motive of self-interest. Even if self-interest is not a good motive, we can still do what's morally right and be motivated by self-interest. The self-interested motive does not make the action morally wrong. It is still morally right. Morally, it is right to sue Chumhum, in order to help our wealthy client, just as it is right to save a drowning person, in order to collect the reward.

It's also possible to do the morally wrong thing from a good motive, such as compassion. However, this does not change the fact that the action is morally wrong. The compassionate motive does not make the action morally right.

If lying is morally wrong, as Alicia believes, then it's morally wrong for Shen Yuan to lie about what happened to him in 2009. It is also morally wrong for Alicia to convince him to lie. Although she does hesitate initially when asked to convince Shen Yuan to lie, she nevertheless convinces him to lie. In the episode in question she is not shown convincing

Shen Yuan to lie. We only hear later on that he has lied, at her convincing.

Shen Yuan's lie is told during negotiation. The case never goes to trial. It would be difficult to imagine Alicia convincing Shen Yuan to lie on the witness stand and to commit perjury. She would be convincing him to lie on the witness stand and commit perjury from the motive of compassion for future victims of torture and imprisonment. This would make her action very similar to that of the Demorys, whom she morally condemned.

Alicia should not have convinced Shen Yuan to lie. As she should well know, a good motive does *not* make a wrong action right.[1]

---

[1] Work on this chapter was supported by a Lenfest Grant from Washington and Lee University in the summer of 2012. I would like to thank H.F. (Gerry) Lenfest, as well as the university, for their generosity. Research was conducted at Yale University and at Washington and Lee University School of Law, using materials from the Wilbur C. Hall Library. This chapter is dedicated to my new nephew, Adam James Thomas Shiel.

IV

Psychobabble

9
Peter's Peter Problem

SKYLER KING AND ROBERT ARP

Peter Florrick is a scumbag. He's a Chicago-style politician who's corrupt, but what *really* makes him lower than low is the fact that he cheated on his wife.

If you take a moment to reflect on all that's entailed in infidelity for the standard married person—lying to and concealing things from your spouse, betraying the promise to be faithful, sharing bodily fluid inside or outside *someone else's* body, the possibility of giving your spouse an STD or HIV you picked up from the affair, the fact that you'll undoubtedly be caught at some point and there'll be tons of anger, sorrow, and regret—you can see how few would object to Peter having his own 'little Peter' Bobbitt-ized. (Recall that in 1993 Lorena Bobbitt cut off half of her husband John's penis while he was sleeping and threw it out of her car window, part of the reason being that he was supposedly a cheating bastard.) Who can forget the scene where Peter and Alicia are making love and Peter's current whore, Amber Madison, calls right in the middle and Peter actually stops and answers the call!?

The creators of *The Good Wife*, Michelle and Robert King, have made it clear in several interviews that Peter's character—and the whole show itself—was inspired by the likes of lying, cheating, SOB politicians like Bill Clinton (a.k.a. Slick Willy), John Edwards, Eliot Spitzer, Dick Morris, and Mark Sanford. These married, male politicians

103

are not alone on the cheating home front. It has been estimated that some fifty-two percent of American men currently living have cheated on their spouses at some point in their marriage by having intercourse with someone else, with the estimate being higher if you count blowjobs and handjobs in the mix.

Men and Their Manly Excuses

So, why do so many men cheat on their wives? There are numerous reasons that have been given by men themselves. One such reason is the ever famous, "My wife has become a cow." This is a fairly common reason, and plenty of men find it hard to have sex with an unattractive partner. This is probably why many women think that guys are "nothing but pigs," or that guys only view women as sex toys.

A second reason given by men is, "There's so much eye candy around." The fact of the matter is that even though there are plenty of cows around, there are also plenty of vixens, too, making for lots of temptation. It doesn't help that Hollywood seems to mandate all its actresses to be 110-pound supermodels. How can men be faithful in a world with so many hotties?

Another reason is, "I see it all of the time on the Playboy Channel." Porn is all over the place—on cable TV, on the Internet, at the local drug store—and oftentimes men are portrayed as cheating on their spouses with either no or even positive consequences. Research shows that porn affects men more than it does women; the primary reason being that men are visual creatures, whereas women tend to be "turned on" by things they have to imagine, such as a sex scene in a book. However, that's not to say that women *don't* look at pornography. Consider Grace in the Season Four episode, "Battle of the Proxies:" she ends the scene by typing "sex" into the Chumhum search engine. Naughty, naughty.

"My wife always has a headache" is another excuse men give. If a woman doesn't give her man enough sex, a lot of times he'll go looking for it elsewhere. Maybe we should blame God for this male feature? After all, he did tell Adam to "be fruitful and multiply," didn't he?

Men also cite, "She's just not kinky enough," as justification for their affairs. Men like to have wild and freaky monkey sex, y'all! Research and plenty of surveys over the past fifty years show that men tend to get bored with the bed life and seek out new things.

The next excuse is, "My friend is a cheater, so I'm in good company." It's easier to cheat if you've got a support system—even if it is based on a logical fallacy. This excuse represents the *ad populum* logical fallacy. *Ad populum* means "argument to the people," and this case exemplifies a particular type of *ad populum* argument: "Well, he's doing it, so I can too."

Perhaps the most prevalent excuse is, "I'll be able to get away with it." Fat chance! It never happens, but men think "I'm different—I won't get caught." But men always do. Along the way in the affair: every time the phone rings you'll jump, fearing that your adulterating cohort is calling; there will be an exponential increase in "late nights at work" or "business trips," followed by an exponential decrease in the desire to have sex with your wife; you'll also start to be more non-communicative with your spouse, prompting her to claim, "Talk to me, Jim" or ask, "What's wrong, Frank?" or "What's going on, John?"

Another pitiful excuse proffered by men is, "I had a moment of weakness." Yeah, right. Thomas Jefferson had a "moment of weakness" when he suffered from dysentery in 1774, which prohibited him from carrying a draft of his *Summary View of the Rights of British America*, a substantial state paper designed to instruct delegates who were to attend the Continental Congress of September 5, 1774, to Williamsburg (luckily his slave pal, Jupiter, was there to deliver the paper for him!). However, to say certain members of the Kennedy family, a family swaddled in affairs, all experienced a "moment of weakness" is completely asinine. You don't stumble into affairs; you deliberately contrive them. The simple truth is you arrive at the consummation of an affair by degrees, progressing from an initial observation of "one smoldering babe" to entertaining thoughts of conversing with her, then to initiating a conversation or perhaps a dinner to spending private time together, and, if you're dumb enough to continue to pursue this course of action, you eventually reach the grand finale of coitus.

Finally, perhaps the most audacious excuse is, "I'm the Emperor of Morocco, so it's the law!" According to some recent DNA research, it has been determined that Moulay Ismail, Emperor of Morocco from 1672 to 1727, had some 888 children. "He was the Henry Ford of mass copulation," claims psychologist Nando Pelusi, and Ismail not only had four wives, but some five hundred concubines he kept jailed until they were thirty years old. How's that for "unchecked primal urges"!?

Of course, if a man wants to cheat bad enough, he can *invent* reasons to justify or seek out a new means for satiating his sex drive. However, don't get the impression that all men are like this. These are merely some of the reasons cheating men use to calm the inexorable beleaguering of their consciences. Cheating just isn't a wise thing to do, and it always ends terribly—unless, of course, you're an untouchable emperor.

In Our Genes, So It's Hard To Keep It in Our Jeans

"You and me baby ain't nothin' but mammals, so let's do it like they do on the Discovery Channel" goes the chorus of Bloodhound Gang's 1999 song, "The Bad Touch." Another reason men—as well as psychologists, therapists, and other researchers—give for why men cheat has to do with the fact that we're animals deep down. After all, we have an evolutionary past, and we can trace that past to a common ancestry with primates, then mammals, then other "lower" life forms.

There's a field of psychology called *evolutionary psychology* that emerged near the end of the 1980s that actually provides an explanation as to why men cheat. Evolutionary psychology is exactly what it sounds like: it's the idea that much of human behavior—though not all, obviously—is the result of brain and psychologically related adaptations that have evolved over millennia to solve recurring problems in our hominid ancestors' environments. In other words, just as *physical* human traits are the result of successful adaptations and mutations that have been beneficial to humans over the course of time, so too, our brains and the resulting *psychological* traits emerging from our brains evolved and adapted to give us the benefits of language, complex problem solving, emotions, and most importantly, consciousness.

For example, you ever wonder why it's so easy for kids to pick up any language, or many languages, so easily? Evolutionary psychologists think that part of the reason is that they have evolved a kind of wired-in language module or intelligence. The same goes for a human's natural ability to be social, or do math, or even detect when something is unjust, like when someone cuts in line or cheats on a test.

From an evolutionary perspective, the most important thing for anything living is survival and the reproduction of offspring. So, it makes sense that males of any species go around trying to impregnate as many females as is possible. This way, the chances of one's genes being passed on is greater. The more offspring a male can have, the better, in this game of sheer survival and perpetuating one's genes we call "life." Our genes, then, help to explain why it's so hard to keep it in our jeans!

Chicks Cheating

Alicia cheated on Peter with Will Gardner after Peter's affair went public. They were separated, but not officially divorced. Women cheat, too, but not as much as men, seemingly. Why? Evolutionary psychologists have come up with something they call the *parental investment theory*. Attempting to have as many children as possible requires a great amount of effort for a woman, given the pregnancy, the caring for the child, the rearing of the child, and many other factors. For men, this isn't an issue, obviously. They can just hit it, and run! So, given the investment of time and energy, women want to make the relationship with their man work and not screw it up by cheating, which oftentimes ends the relationship.

Yet, we all know that women cheat, anyway. The parental investment theory has been challenged by biologists and some evolutionary psychologists who believe that women are genetically programmed to have sex with several different men in order to increase the chances of healthy children with the greatest likelihood of survival. There is now a growing body of evidence that females from across the animal kingdom—including guppies, scorpions, reptiles, mammals, and of course "the birds and the bees"—are promiscuous, cheating little beatches, and researchers say they're convinced human females are the same.

Ring of Gyges

Peter Florrick is a politician not unlike John Edwards, Eliot Spitzer, or Mark Sanford. What do these guys all have in common besides being lying, cheating SOBs? They're all powerful men. There's something to the idea that "absolute power corrupts absolutely," a notion that is discussed in Plato's most famous work, *The Republic*. In Book II, one of the participants in the discussion, Glaucon, tells the story of Gyges of Lydia, who was a mere shepherd in the service of the king of Lydia. Gyges finds a ring in a cave and discovers that the ring gives him the power to become invisible by turning it on his finger. He then proceeds to use his new power of invisibility to seduce the queen, and get her to help him murder the king so he himself can become king. The story is supposed to emphasize the fact that if someone has no fear of being punished (the "absolute power" part), then he or she will do all manner of self-centered, self-serving, and wicked things (the "corrupts absolutely" part).

Now, the question becomes this, which Socrates, Glaucon, and Adeimantus discuss in the rest of *The Republic*: It's easy to see how some scumbag shepherd could do evil things with lots of power, but what about someone who's already a fine, upstanding person? Can a basically good person be corrupted absolutely with absolute power? A lot of people—smart researchers, too—would say, "Hell, yes!" So, if you give a Peter Florrick or a Bill Clinton enough power, he starts to think that the standard rules don't apply to him anymore, including standard *moral* rules like those associated with faithfulness, honesty, and integrity in a marriage.

You Don't Wants to Gits Bobbitt-ized

In the beginning of this chapter we noted that some fifty-two percent of American men currently living have cheated on their spouses at some point in their marriage. Interestingly enough, some ninety percent of the same American men view cheating—to include their own—as something that is wrong and should not occur. There are actually numerous reasons why you shouldn't cheat on your spouse.

First is the simple fact that jealous husbands, wives, or mistresses will kill you. As William Congreve, an English playwright and poet, once said, "Hell hath no fury like a woman scorned" (and, no, Shakespeare didn't coin that term, just in case you were wondering). So, use your advanced reasoning faculties that nature bestowed you with and *avoid* self-inflicted extinction.

Also, there is the matter of the *promise* you made. Now, in our society today, promises might not mean as much as they did, say, sixty years ago, but that doesn't change the fact that the promise of marriage is the biggest and most important promise you ever made. To use dramatic, metaphoric terms, to break the covenant of marriage is "to rend the very fabric of your soul and irreparably sunder the bonds of amity."

Cheating causes harm to your spouse. Besides the potential to transform your spouse into a killer, what *other* effects can cheating have? It dramatically alters your spouse's emotional landscape and psyche. Remember the "irreparably sundering the bonds of amity" part in the last paragraph? Yeah, you were the person your spouse trusted the *most* (hopefully), which means that your spouse's best friend, anchor, confidante, and love just inflicted the greatest wound sufferable—a wound maybe even greater than death, for at least in death your spouse has the comfort of positive, jovial times spent with you, but cheating forever embitters both your spouse's memories of you and perception of marriage and, potentially, the *entire world* (meaning, your spouse might feel like *no one* can be trusted, like *everyone* is a crook or a double-crosser, after you cheat). Nothing can properly articulate the deep sense of betrayal cheating suffuses into the psyche of a spouse.

Not only does cheating affect you and your spouse, it affects your children if you have them. Usually cheating persons are evicted from relationships and marriages, which means little Alicia and Will see less of Mommy or Daddy and eventually learn that Mommy and Daddy are divorced. And they're bound to learn the reason *why* you got divorced. Such harsh sundering causes many to develop extreme anger, bitterness, an inability to form long-lasting or intimate relationships, an inability to trust others, or depression and, in the most extreme cases, suicidal tendencies. You love your children, don't you? Then why would you *ever* contemplate plunging them into the throes of such a torturing maelstrom?

And we also have to consider the harm it brings to your family. Any socially acceptable person or family will irrefutably deem cheating repugnant. So, on top of the fact that your spouse wants to kill you, and you are now a lying, cheating, adulterer who profoundly wounded your spouse's sense of self-worth and trust, *and* your children are likely exhibiting anger commensurate to the Incredible Hulk, you've also wounded *your* family.

Birthmarks, Brazil, and Boners (of Course)

Last, but certainly not least, after surviving everything we discussed up to this point, there remains the fact that you are now *officially* a lying, cheating, SOB. Oh, you better believe that your spouse will have "comfort sessions" with close friends where they all talk about how dastardly, evil, and crass you are; where they delineate the extent and magnitude to which you are a d-bag. Your name will forever be marred with the connotation of adulterer, fornicator, and one-prone-to-infidelity. Basically, both you and your life *suck* afterwards in some way. For example, Eli Gold, Peter's campaign manager, has to field a rather embarrassing question about whether or not Peter has a birthmark shaped like Brazil on his penis in the Season Four episode, "Anatomy of a Joke." There isn't a *good* way for Eli to deny that assertion. See? Peter, that lying, cheating, SOB always has some crazy person coming out of the woods saying, "I had marvelous sex with that man!" Take it vicariously through Peter: you don't want that experience in real life.

Whether it's an asinine justification for cheating, a "power trip" that elicits feelings of invincibility, or an appeal to nature, all the categories we discussed result in the resounding message that cheating *never* yields propitious results. Interestingly enough, from that same evolutionary perspective that got Peter and other men into this mess in the first place, it's actually in our best interest *not* to cheat, if we want to survive in a less-than-miserable existence. Peter's peter problem is patently preventable (How's that for some bitchin' alliteration!?).

Nonetheless, some of you will continue to exist as intransigent apes consumed by your primal desires. Try not to go bananas on anyone during your freaky monkey sex and, also, keep your bananas away from those of us who realize the importance of honoring commitments and fidelity. Who knows? Perhaps one day we'll hear about your peculiar birthmarks on the news. Then those of us contributing to this book can say, "Ha! You lying, cheating, SOB, we *told you so!*"

10
The Death Drive in *The Good Wife*

ROGER HUNT

Murder, rape, torture for pleasure, swindling someone out of their life savings, predatory sexual behavior toward a minor—these all count as examples of evil, with some being more or less evil, obviously. Evil is the malicious, unjust, intentional physical or psychological harm caused to a creature capable of being harmed.

Fact: sometimes people do evil things. Consider the horrible actions of *The Good Wife* character, Colin Sweeney, which are similar to the real-life murder, deception, and manipulation we see documented on shows on the Investigation, Discovery, and Biography channels. Are these people Satan incarnate? Did they suffer as children? Do they lack certain neural connections in their brains? Are they just plain amoral?

One of the many issues facing the viewer is: what are we to do with this evil? Give in to it? Play by its rules? Fight it? *The Good Wife* doesn't admonish evil *wholly*, but rather understands it as part of the real world as something that can be used, rather than resisted. But used how? In general, evil is a choice and should be resisted under most circumstances. I say *most* because the idea of using evil to reach noble ends is not new, and we've all heard that sometimes the "end justifies the means"—where the end is something good while the so-called means has to do with something evil. Nowadays, many would argue that it's evil to torture a terrorist, even if by doing so we can get him to reveal where he hid the bomb. Of course, many would also argue such torture *isn't* evil, given the circumstances!

Evil and Perspective

The Good Wife gives us two views of good and evil. In one case, we observe the law in practice, in particular how messy, petty, and personal it can be. In the other, we observe good and evil in personalities. In the law, there are pretty clear guidelines. At times it's messy, but an acceptable decision is often reached through negotiation, argumentation, and a sound jury. I might call this an idealized or absolute form of evil. Throughout the centuries moral scholars have worked out a set of moral guidelines that we then codify into a set of legal norms. However, we can question the inspiration for those guidelines. Did they come from purely rational investigation? Are they a product of divine command? Did some people get together one day and hash it all out?

In order to develop an absolute moral philosophy, we need a positive answer to these questions. I have trouble accepting any of these answers, and instead prefer to think that the concepts of good and evil begin with us as individuals. When someone judges something to be good or evil, that person is primarily considering how such an action affects her life. It's from those experiences of good and evil that we have since developed the idea of absolute moral laws.

We make generalizations based on our experiences. These generalizations are not always incorrect, at least in the sense that we could find anyone to disagree. A few years ago in Boston, a drug deal went wrong and an infant was murdered in cold blood. I don't think anyone would consider this good, in fact everyone would probably consider it evil. Not all of our responses to events are so clear-cut, but as we engage in discussion, we tend to come around to a judgment that most of us can live with.

Evil and the Death Drive

How do we come to these judgments? Where do the intuitions originate? Contemporary brain science—neuroscience—gives us intriguing answers to these questions. For instance, neuroscientists have found the some of our basic moral instincts are closely associated with the activation of the amygdala, a small peanut-sized part of the brain. There is another, different part of the brain in the cerebral cortex, the outer layer of the brain, which is activated when we consider morality from an abstract perspective.

With the advent of fMRI, we see that our basic moral intuitions occur first in the amygdala area, and then are processed at the abstract level. Unfortunately, neuroscience has only come this far, and there are many speculations about the structure of this process. While the popular atheist writer Sam Harris has argued that these discoveries will lead us to a new science of morality, we only have a few suggestive correlations up to this point.

Prior to the advent of neuroscience, many theorists attempted to explain and understand the processes of moral intuition. One of these theorists was Sigmund Freud. Freud had a wide-ranging knowledge of many areas. A neurologist by training, he also wrote about society, culture, religion, psychology, anthropology, and art. His understanding of the mind came from his ideas about morality.

Freud understood the mind in several ways over the course of his career. One way is his theory in which the mind consists of the id, ego, and super-ego. The id contains the instincts, which motivate the ego (the self), which is carefully supervised by the super-ego. Freud thought of morality as tied to the super-ego, holding down the devilish instincts from the id.

However, I prefer one of Freud's later theories, popularly known as *drive theory*. According to this theory, the human mind is composed of two kinds of motivation, a *life drive* and a *death drive*, or *Eros* and *Thanatos*. We can think of the life drive as motivating us to be with other people, while the death drive motivates us to be away from other people; the extreme of the former being a return to the mother's womb, and the extreme of the latter being death.

Freud described these drives as interacting, or fusing at various levels to create more complicated structures. For example, the action of having sex contains instincts to unite with another, but also to escape. The unite part is simple to grasp. The escape aspect comes from the orgasm, sometimes known as "the little death." The experience is one of extreme euphoria, where the other person almost doesn't exist, at least for a few seconds.

In a healthy person, Freud speculated that the death drive comes into the service of the life drive. Or rather, that the sometimes aggressive and hostile instincts associated with death are used to attain the goals of the life drive. Think of someone who tries desperately hard to impress a date. He is being aggressive, but in a good way.

Problems occur, however, when the relationship is the other way around and the energy of the life drive serves the death drive. We may call this type of mind diseased or pathological, because of the various kinds of destruction those with mental illness or extreme anger may inflict. Think of the theater shooting in Aurora, Colorado or the school shooting in Newtown, Connecticut. These young men were likely motivated to destroy, they did so, and we hope to subject them to the full extent of the law, moral or legal. There are more subtle examples of this pathology; instances where the transgression may not become a legal or medical issue, but still seem evil.

It's this category of evil that's explored so brilliantly in *The Good Wife*. The evil perpetrated isn't absolute in the sense of breaking any moral code, but rather it is evil from the perspective of the other characters. The show gives us three prime examples of pathological or evil characters (life drive in the service of death drive): Louis Canning (Michael J. Fox); Peter Florrick (Chris Noth); and, my favorite, Colin Sweeney (Dylan Baker).

The Structure of a Case

We'll look at these three characters as psychiatric *cases*. A case has three parts: description, dynamics, and drives.

- First, *describing* the person: What feelings does he report? What is our experience of him? What kind of person does he seem like?

- Second, the *dynamics*: What kind of relationship is he in? How does he interact with other people? What kinds of things does he buy? Where does he spend his free time?

- Finally, making inferences about the fusion of his *drives*: Is the life drive or the death drive dominant? Are his impulses mature or child-like? Does he repeat any particular scenarios? What motivates her?

The conclusion of each case will have two parts:

1. Do the drives fuse in a way that favors the life drive, the death drive, or is neutral between them? (It's doubtful whether anyone achieves the third—maybe the Dalai Lama, but more likely only Buddha or Jesus achieved this level of Enlightenment.)

2. Do the drives discharge (stimulate action, feelings, or thoughts) at low, medium, or high levels? This refers to the kind of pleasure we get from the drive achieving its aim. Pleasure in marriage or having children would be high; making friends would be medium; and manipulating others would be low; sadistic pleasure would be the lowest (at least according to Freud in *Beyond the Pleasure Principle*).

Colin Sweeney

Description: Colin Sweeney is introduced to us as the CEO of an investment fund, and he has been accused of his wife's murder. He immediately evokes that creepy tingle one gets from a true weirdo. Alicia visits his apartment and he shows her a grotesque painting, making her, and I bet most of the audience very uncomfortable. He always makes these creepy stares and smiles which make it seem like he's hiding something or putting one over on the lawyers and the judge. We continuously see a brooding, self-serving maniac, out to save himself or to pull the wool over someone else's eyes. I once heard someone say that ten percent of CEO's are pathological; Sweeney certainly seems to fit this mold at face value.

Dynamics: While Colin Sweeney certainly seems to have an inherent knack for dealing with, motivating, and manipulating other people, he also seems to lack any kind of deep connection to them. Even his wife's death hardly fazed him. At one point, we see Sweeney exhibit some feelings for Alicia, but we later realize that he was capitalizing on the predispositions of her own character (which are the focus of the show). He's a man who seems to be absolutely devoid of any deep relationships, and he likes it that way.

Drives: Would we say that Sweeney is more likely to be motivated to *be-with* or *be-without* others? Intuitively, the answer is *be-without*. It also seems that his actions, feelings, and lack of relationships support this. Any chance for him to get close to someone is immediately curtailed by his ulterior, often insidious, motives. Sweeney represents the most basic form of *being-without*, or the death drive. He seems to get a basic kind of pleasure from seeing people in pain, much like the rest of us might get from getting married or eating really, really, really good chocolate cake (note to my wife: I said really, really, really good). All of his life drive energy is in the service of fulfilling this sadistic pleasure, or helping him to escape punishments that might defer such pleasure.

Sweeney is not mentally ill in any sense of the term. He's not behaviorally unpredictable, socially deterred, nor neurologically disabled. It is as though there is no internal life for Sweeney, except when he needs to escape punishment, in which case he can feign being a person. Sweeney's drives fuse in a way that's primarily directed towards the death drive and discharge at the lowest level, except when he is threatening, in which case they discharge at a low level.

Peter Florrick

Description: The show begins with Peter apologizing for his infidelity. However, it's not clear then, nor is it ever clear later, whether Peter's feelings of remorse come from genuine guilt or political damage control. It is always ambiguous: sometimes it seems like he genuinely has feelings, other times not. It seems likely that Peter may not be fully aware either. He always seems conflicted, torn between saving his marriage or his career. His feelings are never clear. On the other side, he demonstrates a particular ability to discover plots. He has a piercing intellect, oftentimes directed towards revenge. I do not want him as an enemy.

Dynamics: Peter seems to love Alicia and his children very much. He shows pride in watching his children, especially his son, grow up. While his actions deserve hatred from those around him, others still see good in him, or at least opportunity. Even Alicia is weakened by his charms (and circumstance), and decides to be with him on the campaign trail. We can't overlook his mother, who treats him like some kind of glass doll that needs to be protected, and her efforts trickle down to the children (not in an effort to help them, but ultimately to help Peter). It's like Peter has a kind of protective barrier around him composed of many different people (Eli, Jackie, Alicia, Cary, the DNC) who are not trying to protect him, but simply following their own hearts. At the same time, Peter always has some enemy, which makes this barrier necessary. What often appears as a 'lucky escape' is usually a confluence of random factors geared towards saving him from danger.

Drives: Peter is ambivalent, well protected, and has enemies: textbook paranoia. Does this mean that Peter is motivated to *be-with* or *be-without*? The safest places for a paranoid person is away from everyone. The second safest place is locked in a castle with servants protecting him. I think we find Peter in the latter, politics; the former would be a mental institution. While Peter's drives fuse in a way that favors the death drive and discharging at the mid-level: he is able to develop the kinds of relationships required to protect him from the evil (Childs, Scott-Carr, Kresteva in his view) surrounding him, but unable to truly honor or develop a mutual fulfillment in them. His relationships are designed to protect him.

Louis Canning

Description: The first thing we notice about Canning (and the first thing he brings to our attention) is his neurological disorder, tardive dyskinesia, which makes it difficult to speak at times while also causing involuntary movements. He's extremely charming and has a beautiful family. He is ambitious and loves a challenge, often taking on cases of those whom we might intuitively suspect to be guilty. He has a brilliant track record in the courtroom (except against Alicia). His legal strategies are intricate, well disguised, and ruthless.

Dynamics: We do not know much about Canning's personal life except for when Alicia visits his home and meets his beautiful wife and children. He has a kind of kindred spirit in the insurance lawyer woman, who always uses her baby to disrupt negotiations, in an effort to take down Lockhart Gardner. He seems to have a relationship of mutual respect with Alicia, but also seems to negotiate in good faith only to go back on his word. As with Peter, it's not clear whether Louis wants relationships to further his own ends, or if he wants to develop something more lasting. It is clear, however, that whenever he does begin to establish trust with someone, he makes that person regret it.

Drives: There is a psychoanalytic theory about narcissism, which goes against popular wisdom. We often think of the narcissist as someone in love with himself. Someone who does whatever it takes to reach their own goals despite whomever they have to upset. Conversely, psychoanalytic theory talks about narcissism as self-hate. The true narcissist, not the sociopath, works so hard to protect others that he ultimately destroys himself, for if the other were ever to become deeply involved with him, that person would ultimately be disappointed (in the narcissist at least, as the narcissist hates himself).

Psychosomatics

There is another related branch of medicine: psychosomatics. This branch, which has recently gained status in German medical schools, presents the view that one's mind, or psychic structure, has the capacity to create physical symptoms. We have all felt back pain or headaches, when we worry about finishing an assignment or making the sales quota, right? At a more extreme level, psychosomatics holds that cancer and other very serious medical and neurological disorders can be caused by various kinds of mental stress. We simply don't know enough about the mind-brain-body relationship to make any definitive claims about what is purely physical and what is purely mental, in fact most philosophers don't even recognize a difference between mental and physical.

Canning's neurological disorder may be the result of the kind of self-attack we see in schizophrenia, in other words, turning aggression against the self. Were he to let this self-attack completely take over, he might become schizophrenic. Instead, he is able to function successfully, relegating his self-attacks to the brain's motor cortex (I presume). He has even found a way to use that disruption in motor control to further the more socially adaptive ends of winning settlements. His drives fuse favoring the death-drive, but discharge at a very high level.

Evil Is Everywhere

Evil is everywhere and comes in many forms. *The Good Wife* explores evil from a more and realistic pragmatic point of view, and this is one reason why the show is so fascinating. Evil can be well disguised on the show, no doubt, and in many cases we viewers (and often the characters in the series) are persuaded to empathize with the evildoers or those who attempt to commit immoral acts. It's our death drive, however, that accounts for much of the evil we perpetrate in this world.

V

A Balancing Act

11
Can a Good Wife Have It All?

JENNIFER SWANSON

While it's not every day that women find themselves in the news because their husbands have been caught on camera sucking the toes of a call girl, it's a pretty common occurrence for women to face the question of whether or not they can "have it all."

The Good Wife's Alicia Florrick is dealing with both. When her husband, Illinois State's Attorney Peter Florrick, is thrown in jail on charges of corruption, Alicia has to return to work to support their teenage children, Zach and Grace. According to the US Bureau of Labor Statistics, in 2010 over seventy percent of mothers were in the labor force. That's a lot of women who are both working and raising a family just like Alicia is now. So we have to ask: is it possible to have it all?

Throwing Yourself Fully into It

Alicia returns to work not because she wants to, but because she has to. And it's a good thing she caught Will Gardner's attention at Georgetown, because otherwise it would have probably been very difficult to find a job after more than a decade out of the work force. Alicia is hired and immediately thrust into a competition with another new hire—the fresh-out-of-law-school Cary Agos. After a six-month audition for the one permanent position available, the partners will decide which one to let go. This means that there's no time to ease her way back into working again. Alicia has to throw herself fully into it from the get-go.

It's not clear, though, if this is going to be the start of a new life for Alicia or just a temporary detour from the mommy track. It's probably not even clear to her at that point. Peter tells her, "Thanks for playing the breadwinner for a while. It's not going to last forever." But is Peter going to get out of jail? If he does, will he stop banging prostitutes? Can she forgive him for the banging that has already occurred? These are important questions but Alicia doesn't have the answers yet. So for the moment, she has to take her new situation seriously.

This means that Alicia can no longer be a full-time mom, so she enlists Peter's mother, Jackie, for help. Jackie spends a couple of hours a day at the Florrick house after Zach and Grace get out of school. Sometimes she stays late to make dinner; some days she stays until after the kids have gone to bed because Alicia is still at work. It's clear that Alicia is not happy with the situation (especially since Jackie is a classic meddling mother-in-law). But she's also finding it difficult to be less involved with her kids than she's used to.

In the Season One episode "Painkiller," she hires a nanny, Molly, but quickly fires her after discovering that she talked to Grace about the HPV vaccine. Having seen pictures of Peter smoking crack with a hooker on Zach's computer, Molly tells Alicia, "You don't know what's going on in your own home." Three episodes later, in "Bang," Will pulls Alicia off a big case just after Peter is released from jail. When she asks why, he tells her, "I just thought with Peter coming home, your life's complicated enough. I should give you a break." In Season Two's "Bad Girls," new partner Derek Bond institutes a peer review policy. He advises Alicia that her co-workers think she keeps "leisurely hours." So while the nanny clearly thinks Alicia should spend more time with her kids, her peers think she should spend more time at work and her boss thinks she needs time to deal with her husband's return from jail. Is it all too much?

The Good Husband

The show's called *The Good Wife* because it's about, well, Alicia—the wife. But what about Peter? Is he a good husband? The answer to this question is clearly no. But why do we think that? "Because he slept with a prostitute!" is what you're probably yelling right now. "Eighteen times! Not to mention Kalinda! And who knows who else?" So that's our big red flag against Peter—he's a cheating husband. He hasn't been *faithful*. He hasn't been *honest*. He's not *trustworthy*. He isn't *temperate* regarding his sexual desires. He didn't tell Alicia about his one-night stand with Kalinda because he didn't have the *courage*. Not only is Peter not a good husband, he doesn't even seem like a good person, either.

According to Aristotle, one of the great ancient Greek philosophers, being a good person is a matter of being *virtuous*. Virtues are dispositions, or tendencies, to behave in particular ways. We can think of them as demonstrations of our character. If someone is honest on one occasion, that doesn't make him an honest person. An honest person is someone for whom honesty is the norm—for whom telling the truth is just so ingrained that he does it automatically.

Contrary to how we might think of "virtue" today, Aristotle's view was that not all virtues are related to morality. He draws a distinction between *moral virtues* and *intellectual virtues*. Moral virtues are the kinds of things that Peter is lacking. Intellectual virtues are things like knowledge and wisdom. This seems like a good distinction to make because it sounds funny to us to think of it being "right" to have knowledge or wisdom and "wrong" not to. But there's no doubt that being knowledgeable and wise makes our lives better.

So it's not the case that the study of ethics is simply the study of what's right and wrong. That's the study of morality. The study of ethics goes further—it delves into the question of what constitutes *the good life*, or what kind of life it's good for us to have. This sounds like something we would want, right? But we need more than just the moral virtues to have it. As we just said, knowledge and wisdom are part of the good life, and so are things like resourcefulness, prudence, or perseverance. We can also include friendship, a good family life, and career fulfillment. We can call all of these elements that make up the good life *values*.

Peter seems to be missing several of the moral virtues—including faithfulness, honesty, and courage. We might want to say, though, that this doesn't make Peter all bad. Okay, he might be short a few virtues here and there, but surely he has some of them! Isn't this a possibility? For Aristotle, the answer is no.

Virtues

Aristotle believed that in order to fully possess any single virtue, you had to possess them all. This is called the *unity of the virtues*. For example, you can't be fully kind unless you're also fully respectful. When we first encounter Jackie, she seems kind. After all, she's taking on some of the burden of caring for two teenagers because her son's in jail. She obviously loves her grandchildren and she feels compassion for what they (and Alicia) are going through.

But as the series progresses, we start to doubt whether Jackie is really all that kind. From taking the kids to the jail on Peter's birthday behind Alicia's back in Season One, to snooping through her daughter-in-law's lingerie in Season Three, Jackie demonstrates an appalling lack of respect for Alicia. The more apparent it becomes that Jackie is lacking the virtue of respectfulness, the more we lose our belief that Jackie is kind.

Because virtues are demonstrations of our character, a perfectly good character will be perfect in all the virtues. To be lacking in one or more of the virtues displays a defect in our character, and a person with a defective character cannot demonstrate perfection in any particular virtue. A perfectly good person, a virtuous person, is one who has all the virtues and has them all to the fullest extent.

We can expand this idea to values. Values are components of the good life. The recipe for a perfect life, then, is to have all the values, and have them all to their fullest extents.

Sounds easy, right? Well, maybe not. Having to be fully prudent, fully resourceful, fully wise—it sounds exhausting. In fact, it seems pretty much impossible. And not only is it impossible in practice, it is also impossible *in principle*. Trying to achieve the perfect life is like trying to make 2 + 2 = 5. It simply can't be done.

Let's talk about tact and frankness. Both are values. So according to Aristotle, we can only be perfectly frank if we're perfectly tactful, and vice versa. But is it possible to be perfectly tactful *and* perfectly frank? It doesn't seem so. Think about Eli Gold. Eli is practically the embodiment of frankness. Because of this, it surprises us when he doesn't just speak his mind with no regard for other people's feelings. Any demonstration of tact simply seems out of character for him. If we admit that Eli is very close to being perfectly frank, how is he supposed to fit in all this tact that Aristotle would want him to display?

We can say something similar about Kalinda Sharma. Just as Eli is the epitome of frankness, Kalinda is the epitome of discretion. While this is a positive attribute with regard to her job as an investigator, it hinders the development of friendships because she's unable to be open with other people. Her friendship with Alicia seems a bit one-sided because Kalinda never opens up—no matter how many tequila shots she's had. She embodies the value of discretion but fails entirely with the value of openness. At the end of Season Three, Alicia and Kalinda are together at the bar when Kalinda suddenly says, "I'm not gay. I'm flexible." It seems to come out of nowhere, but really she's just answering Alicia's question. You know, the one she asked two years ago. Is she going to be more open with Alicia as the series progresses? We don't know, but insofar as she is, she loses the value of discretion as she gains the value of openness.

Perfectly Impossible

Moral philosopher Michael Slote, in his book *The Impossibility of Perfection*, addresses these questions and introduces the idea of *partial values*. Partial values are paired concepts that seem to contradict one another. Slote uses tactfulness and frankness as examples of partial values—"to have either one of them is to be in a less than ideal situation vis-à-vis the other." In other words, when we're frank, we have compromised our tactfulness, and vice versa. Same thing goes for openness and discretion.

Slote's ideas about partial values arose from his study of psychologist Carol Gilligan's groundbreaking book *In a Different Voice: Psychological Theory and Women's Development*. In this book, Gilligan discusses the relationship between gender and morality. It used to be the case that this idea of "the good life" was perceived differently for men and women. Values such as achievement, accomplishment, and recognition were seen as male-oriented, while other values, such as friendship, love, and relationships were seen as female-oriented.

What Slote came to realize is that there are several paired partial values that match up to this traditional gendered view. He uses the example of adventure and security. Adventure has traditionally been seen as more of a masculine thing while women have been thought to need security. Nowadays, though, it is much more widely recognized that women as well as men benefit by being adventurous and men are equally as in need of security as women. It's clear that Alicia needs some adventure in her life and Peter perhaps needs to focus more on security. There is something lacking in both their lives.

Another set of partial values that have usually been considered gender-relative are career and family. It was traditionally thought that men find fulfillment through a career while women are best able to find fulfillment within the home. Furthermore, it was considered a bad thing for women to have to work; it took them out of the home. Men were not believed to be worse off for having a wife and children, but the idea that being a stay-at-home father could be a satisfying life was laughable. While stay-at-home fathers haven't quite made it into the mainstream yet, women make up about half the workforce in the United States.

Now you might be asking: Isn't this good? Doesn't this show that women really *can* have it all? Well, no. Because career and family are partial values, the more one is gained, the more the other is lost. The woman (and man) who tries to be a perfect worker as well as the perfect parent is doomed to failure. It just doesn't work that way.

In the Season One episode "Running," Peter is about to hold a press conference to announce that he intends to run for State's Attorney and Alicia is laying down some ground rules. "I don't want the kids involved." Peter agrees. Then she says, "I want to work," and Peter replies that he also wants her to work. They both know that without her support, Peter cannot be elected, but that she needs something of her own as well. She can't just be a stay-at-home mom any longer. Unfortunately, though, there's no way for her to do this that doesn't involve sacrifice both for home and career.

In Season Three, Alicia is working to find out what turned an almost certain not-guilty verdict into a guilty one while at the same time trying to get her kids into Capstone Private School ("What Went Wrong"). Diane wants her to check into the possibility that a juror was updating her blog during deliberations, but she and Peter are meeting with the principal. When Diane asks her where she is, she says, "A prior engagement. I'll be right in." To which Diane replies, "Let's talk when you get back." Her expression tells us that she's not pleased that Alicia isn't available.

Later, Diane mentions that Alicia has been "distracted." Alicia tells her that some "home issues" have come up, but that they have been dealt with. Diane then says, "I want you to get serious about the partner track. I've been watching you. You have it in you. But you can't get distracted. Not with family, not with friendships. Here. You have to keep your eye on the ball." Of course, as Alicia points out, she has a family and she can't change that. But she can decide where to prioritize and where to cut corners.

Career, Family, and More . . .

Alicia's situation is shown most starkly in the Season Three episode "Parenting Made Easy," when she's juggling work, family, and her affair with Will. At one point, she's having dinner with Louis Canning to discuss a settlement in a case. Referencing the job offers he has made Alicia in the past, he says, "You're coming to my firm, Alicia." "I am? When?" "Eventually. Will Gardner and Diane Lockhart don't have children. I do." "And that matters why?" "They like their employees to work long hours because their work is their home. My home is my home. I love my home. I like my kids. If you want to spend more time with your kids, you should be at my firm."

As the food arrives, Canning points out to Alicia that her phone is blinking. She sees that she has twelve missed calls—all from Grace. When she can't reach her daughter, a frantic search begins. Of course, Grace was totally fine; she was simply off getting baptized by a teenager who preaches online. And the twelve calls? Butt-dials.

Alicia realizes that she's not focusing enough on her kids and this leads her to break things off with Will. When she walks into his office, he knows why she's there before she can say anything. She tells him she will miss him, but "it's too much." Now, this makes viewers who are on Team Peter happy, but is this what's best for Alicia? I know a lot of people would say yes—clearly she needs to spend more time with her kids. But are things really so dire? If it hadn't been for the twelve butt-dials, she would have never known that Grace was "missing" because she was never *really* missing. Now, perhaps the very fact that this teenage online preacher was baptizing Grace without Alicia knowing is something to be concerned about. But is it enough to justify Alicia jettisoning her sex life?

If being a working mother is hard, it must be even harder to deal with being a working mother who's also having an outside relationship. And it hardly needs to be said that if something needs to go, the relationship has to be what gets cut. The question is whether it's necessary to cut anything. Doesn't Alicia have a right to her own personal life? After her friendship with Kalinda ends, we never see her hanging out with anyone other than her brother, Owen. Is this okay?

Once we start throwing other elements into the equation (relationships, friendships, hobbies) then it necessarily becomes more complicated. It's impossible to do everything that we want to do. But there are some basics that we shouldn't be denying ourselves. These are things that make up the good life and we shouldn't reject any of them entirely. Of course Alicia needs a social life, and hot sex with the boss isn't bad either.

I Just Want to Be a Mom

Not everyone handles the impossibility of having it all in the same way that Alicia does. Diane has neither a husband nor children, which is of course one way to do it. (Will isn't a family man either, for what it's worth.) Caitlin D'arcy takes a different approach. A rapidly rising young attorney, she shocks Diane by giving notice almost immediately after receiving a promotion. Alicia comes into Diane's office while they're talking, and Diane tells her the news. Alicia is surprised: "But why, Caitlin? I thought you were liking it here." "Oh, I am— so much. I just . . . I got the results back two weeks ago. I'm pregnant! I'm getting married!" Diane tries to explain that this doesn't mean Caitlin needs to quit. "We have a generous maternity leave package and child care and several telecommuting options." Caitlin's reply? "I really am grateful, really I am. I just want to be a mom."

Diane and Caitlin have made different choices, but each has chosen to pursue one path to the exclusion of the other. It certainly appears as though Caitlin's making a mistake. However, she also seems to have a certain insight. Alicia tells her later that she doesn't need to choose between career and family: "There's no reason why you can't work, be a wife and a mother." Caitlin responds, "But I *want* to choose. Maybe it's different for my generation, but I don't have to prove anything. Or, if I have to, I don't want to." In giving up the fight to have it all, Caitlin seems like she may have a better grasp of the realities of life than either Alicia or Diane, yet she still comes across as doing just that—giving up.

What do we want to say about this? Well, for one thing we can be relieved to know that Caitlin won't spend her life struggling against the impossibility of having it all. Or can we? Alicia made the same choice two years out of law school, and look at her now. She's trying her best to balance a career and a family—and it's undoubtedly been more difficult because she spent more than a decade out of the work force. But suppose that Caitlin's situation is different. Suppose that she gets married, has children, and is never under any financial pressure to return to work. Is Caitlin better off than she would have been had she stayed at Lockhart/Gardner?

It's hard to know. Just because perfection is impossible to achieve doesn't mean that we should simply throw up our hands and retreat to safety. I believe both Aristotle and Slote would tell Caitlin that the fuller her life is, the better it will be. By shutting herself off from the possibility of personal fulfillment through a career, Caitlin is not doing herself any favors. We need *balance*. We shouldn't react to the reality that we can't be both perfectly adventurous and perfectly prudent by becoming a daredevil. And just as it's not good for Alicia to be without friendships and romance, it's probably not good for Caitlin to deny herself the obvious joy she gets out of being a lawyer.

You Can't Have It All

When Alicia returned to work, it wasn't clear if it was going to be a permanent thing or if she would go back to being a full-time mother if Peter got out of jail. As the series goes on, it becomes more and more apparent that Alicia loves her job and, while we wouldn't want to say that she regrets the years she spent not working, she has no intention of giving it up. She makes this explicit in the episode "Foreign Affairs." As the State's Attorney election approaches, Wendy Scott-Carr's husband has given a spousal interview and Eli is pressuring Alicia to do the same. At first she resists. She doesn't want to do it and uses her job as an excuse, telling Eli, "Even if I wanted to, I work."

Eventually, however, Alicia changes her mind and decides to do the interview. Eli helps her prepare. "So, tell me about your work. Do you worry that your work takes you away from your children?" "I do, but I needed to work to support my family." "So will you stop working when he's elected?" "No. I care about my work, I care about my clients, and I think that my children support what I do."

Alicia is telling us point-blank that her life includes both family and career and that's how she intends for it to stay. At the same time, *The Good Wife* is telling us that Alicia can't have it all. But even though it's impossible for her to have a perfect life, it's important that she try to make it the best life it can be.

12
Bringing Home the Bacon

KAREN ADKINS

Working moms can recognize their own lives when they watch Alicia Florrick. The distinctive blend of compromise and chaos is as present in the Florrick kitchen as it is in kitchens of working parents across the country. While Alicia regularly can be seen conscientiously handing nutritious bowls of oatmeal to her children in the morning, her Rachael Ray cookbook is front-and-center in her kitchen, and last-minute pizza or takeout is prominent in the Florrick dinner rotation.

The show regularly explores the realities and challenges of combining a professional career with raising a family, often with subtlety as well as humor. And it sometimes speaks in a feminist voice about the hypocrisy of our attitudes towards working mothers. This relative progressivism of the show makes its bland endorsement of so-called "choice feminism" all the more scream-at-your-television worthy.

She Works Hard for the Money

Feminists have long noted the way sexism constrains women's choices. Betty Friedan's pioneering feminist work *The Feminist Mystique* (1963) argued that social expectations led women to think they were choosing a domestic life of motherhood, when in fact they were merely fulfilling unspoken cultural expectations about what proper women *ought* to do with their lives. This life, while appealing in the short run when the babies are small, cute, and sleep a lot, left many women unfulfilled and disconnected in the long run: teenagers trade in hanging out with mom for hanging out with friends, a domestic-only life makes it difficult to connect with a spouse as an sexual partner, and the lack of intellectual challenges and stimulation of the daily chores leaves her feeling bored and like an appliance.

Alicia Florrick's life shows these tensions. When Alicia talks about her prior domestic life, it's generally from a position of distance: she talks as if she were another person entirely. In the very first episode, when mother-in-law Jackie calls Alicia because she wants to know when Alicia's coming home for the hot dinner she made, Alicia laughs and says Jackie sounds like her. When she and Kalinda return to Highland Park for a case during the first season, and Kalinda expresses astonishment that Alicia could have ever lived in such a Stepfordesque suburb, Alicia merely responds, "I liked it at the time" ("Home"). Later in the episode, Alicia also briskly dismisses her former best friend's attempt to resuscitate their friendship; this is clearly no longer her world, and happily so. Her dismissal seems unsurprising; in the second season, she describes her old life with her "mom friends" thinly, as one occupied with conversations about weight ("Ham Sandwich").

In the realm of feminist work and family debates, the classic justification for staying at home is both the exorbitant cost of childcare, and the long hours that professional careers demand. Someone has to stay home so we can save on childcare and at the same time ensure that someone else has career advancement—and that someone is usually the woman and that someone else is the man.

Alicia lives this trajectory. The show makes clear that while she was initially a highly promising attorney (more highly ranked in her Georgetown class than either Will Gardner or Peter, and billed lots of hours at her firm), she decided early on to sacrifice her career, for the sake of Peter's political prospects and for raising the children. She made the feminine move of dependence, and now must unmake it fifteen years later, but with a catch: her former choice to be a stay-at-home mom constrains her current and future choices with demands and responsibilities.

Zach and Grace, her teenage kids, don't go away with her decision to go back to work. We see some of the costs of this choice in Season Three, when Alicia misses the depth of Grace's newfound Christianity ("Parenting Made Easy"). Her struggle to get a position in the law firm, which we later learn she won on connections over merit ("Marthas and Caitlins"), reveals the way in which an apparently simple choice can completely constrain later options.

A Choice or a Hobby?

The dangerous underbelly of calling major economic and life decisions simply *choices* ends up diminishing their seriousness. If working is merely one choice among many, and equally as viable as not working, then work is no longer something sustaining or meaningful. Work becomes something one does either entirely for money (to be done under extreme necessity only), or more like a hobby. I am a college professor now, but maybe later, when I'm bored or rich, I'll take up bowhunting.

Sociologist Thorstein Veblen reminded us over a century ago that the emergence of the stay-at-home wife was a classic marker of the accumulation of wealth for public display of economic power. A wife not working demonstrates to society that her husband is successful and makes enough income for both of them to be comfortable. In this way, work for women was reduced to purely money and status terms rather than something that could be enjoyed or intellectually beneficial; if she didn't need to work, she wouldn't at all.

Alicia's obvious talents and the pleasure she takes in her legal work are similarly undermined by Peter, Jackie, and Cary. We see Peter in jail, thanking her for "playing the breadwinner for a while" ("Pilot"). During his appeal, Peter condescendingly tells her he's happy she's making a life for herself because it gives her a "break" from mommying ("Fixed"). Later, when Peter's political fortunes improve, he slyly notes that if he becomes head of the Democratic Committee he'll earn enough that Alicia wouldn't have to work ("Bad Girls"). And in front of Alicia, Peter condescendingly asks Will "how she's doing at work," in a tone that sounds more like a bemused father asking about his daughter's first full-time job, than a husband whose wife has saved his children from poverty ("Heart").

When the firm puts Alicia and Cary in competition with each other for a single associate's position, Cary condescendingly assumes the Alicia doesn't need the job, telling her she'll have something to fall back on ("Fleas"). During the Season Three battles for the old Florrick home, Jackie makes her resentment of the working Alicia, who refused to be economically controlled by Jackie, clear: "You left," Jackie says accusingly ("Pants on Fire"). The people who surround Alicia simply can't assume she likes what she does, and would want to do it even if she didn't "need" the money.

Kids Are Women's Business

For people like Peter and Cary, women shouldn't need to work because their hands are full raising children, which is always and only a woman's job. Jackie, Alicia's mother-in-law, expresses this viewpoint perfectly towards the end of Season One, when she describes the wife's role: "we stay in the shadows, we comfort, we nurse, but we're always there" ("Hybristophilia"). Alicia's look of revulsion as she listens to this nonsense is priceless. But why do so many people assume that kids are women's business, anyway?

Philosopher Linda Hirshman wrote a zippy critique of "choice feminism," *Get to Work* (2006), arguing that woman who abandoned the workforce to be stay-at-home moms were settling for less-flourishing, smaller lives. She pointed out that nobody asks whether or not men can combine paid work with raising a family; men aren't assumed to be less committed to their children because they leave the house every day for a job. In other words, women are claiming a free choice of a private-only life, but it is both a constrained, and a constraining choice.

So-called 'choices' of working or not are apparently only options for women, not men. It is women's salaries, not men's, that are entirely pitted against the costs of childcare. Men are assumed to be able to, indeed to have to, combine work with family. Finally, the institutional and social pressures that make it hard for any parent to combine a demanding professional job with a family end up tilting the scales for women who are combining a professional and familial life.

Women are disproportionately expected to be present for the school conferences, and handle school holidays and snow days, and then judged for not clocking endless hours at a desk or being truly committed to the job. When the kids are sick, it's Mom who is expected to be at home nursing them to health, not dad, and at the same time she is chastised for taking the time off. It's a no-win situation. Indeed, Alicia's resistance to Will's advances at the end of Season One is all about this cool pragmatism. "Poetry's easy," she tells him over a phone message, "It's the PTA conferences that are hard" ("Running").

What's dishonest in the discussion about feminist battles for workplace equity, specifically the fight for women to have the right to 'choose' between work and home life, is in the word *choice*. There isn't really a choice here given the pressures involved from society and the institutions offering jobs; women are expected to sacrifice for family, *period*—no if, ands, or buts. The workplace pressures range across the spectrum; working-class women don't get to choose their work hours; managers give them shifts to suit company preferences. Professional schedules do not match school and daycare schedules, and as many feminists note, women who take the 'off-ramp' into the home are pulled up short at how difficult reentry to the professional workforce is. Their educations and experience lose value for the time spent in the home.

And yet, when women assert those choices, they are often faced with a double standard. Alicia successfully uses a counter-offer from Louis Canning's firm to negotiate a bigger raise for herself (one she needs so that she can buy a house). While Diane ultimately supports Alicia's aggressive move (indeed, standing up to the other partners to unilaterally give Alicia the raise), her initial defensive response reflects the double standard. She chastises Alicia for her lack of loyalty to Lockhart Gardner, then tells her that either the firm gets more time to decide or Alicia must quit immediately ("Gloves Come Off"). When Alicia, serving on a panel reviewing a police shooting, questions a witness (something the other six male members don't do), she's immediately challenged by two of the other members. One condescendingly tells her that she "doesn't need to be clever," while another says dismissively, "We're not the cops, honey" ("Blue Ribbon Panel"). It's hard not to suspect that a male lawyer wouldn't get such gendered dismissal for aggression (indeed, might even get praised for being assertive). We often see the ways in which women both need to be aggressive to succeed in the workforce, and yet are judged unfeminine or condescended to for those very efforts.

Non-Working Girl

Strangely enough, it's Alicia, of all people, who ends up voicing the rhetoric of choice feminism. When Caitlin d'Arcy (or "Alicia Lite," as Eli Gold refers to her) announces her resignation from the firm because she is pregnant and engaged, Alicia is tasked by Diane Lockhart to talk her out of leaving ("Long Way Home"). After praising Caitlin for her legal skills, Alicia indirectly makes the argument against economic dependency by telling Caitlin that even if she sacrifices work she loves and is good at for someone who's important to her, she may come to regret that decision.

After having seen three seasons of Alicia's anger at being dismissed, diminished, or used by people who saw her as just a housewife or simply an appendage of her husband, and her impressively resuscitated legal skills (which clearly give her pleasure, even as the constraints of the job frustrate her), we know she means this. But Caitlin will not be persuaded, because while she likes her job, she "loves" her fiancé and the emphasis is deliberate here; Caitlin sounds more like a moony teenager in this line than the capable lawyer we've watched. Most crucially, she says that she wants to choose between being a wife and mother, and a lawyer because she doesn't have to, or want to, prove anything to anyone. Alicia refuses to argue with her.

When Diane and Alicia discuss the finality of Caitlin's decision, Diane expresses her feminist disappointment; the glass ceiling wasn't shattered for women to make wedding invitation lists surreptitiously at work. Caitlin has consistently been portrayed as a less substantial version of Alicia, and Diane predicts that she'll be back in fifteen years, like Alicia. Alicia both blandly endorses choice feminism, saying that the glass ceiling probably was broken for choices like Caitlin's, and says that she doesn't think Caitlin will be back.

This seems to be a completely out-of-character pronouncement for Alicia. The periodic flashbacks and references to Alicia and Peter's early marriage tell us that they were passionate in their young years (even as he was the philandering state's attorney); this, along with the fifty-percent divorce rate, might make Alicia at least as skeptical as Diane about the possibility of romantic passion outlasting any need for remunerative work. Because divorce rates, and the disconcerting reality that otherwise healthy partners can lose their jobs or get sick or even die, sacrificing earning power is a risky game for women, as Alicia herself knows all too well.

Even if Alicia doesn't want to talk about depressing economic realities, it's surprising that she doesn't raise the other social issues around marriage. Betty Friedan's point that a domestic life limits a woman (children grow up) was about more than economics. We certainly see the arc of fulfillment and boredom back and forth played out in Alicia's marriage.

The working Alicia we see is assertive, she often gets angry with Peter over his assumptions, at times she becomes sexually aggressive with him, and she is an active voice in the negotiations concerning his return from jail to her apartment ("Bad").

Her assertiveness is matched by Peter's persistent surprise and resistance—this is clearly a new Alicia. It doesn't seem like a stretch to guess that before his imprisonment, their marriage was a pretty conventional separate-spheres arrangement. Alicia herself describes it that way, pointing out to Peter that their old marriage featured him at work all the time, and her at home ("Foreign Affairs"). Peter was the breadwinner and had authority in big decisions; Alicia kept the house and children running. Alicia clearly recognizes the way in which she's no longer the contented housewife she was; Alicia's life is almost schizophrenically sequenced. She spent fifteen years as the quintessentially happy homemaker and society mother, then did a complete about-face to become a billable-hours-mindful law associate at a big firm.

We see in Alicia's periodic handling of divorce cases that she gets her chance to express some feminist irritation with dismissive husbands and the traditional notions of marital roles. To use one example among many, "let us be angry for you," she tells Caroline Wilder, when she is abandoned by her rock star husband for a younger model ("Unplugged"). By the time Peter's campaign for re-election to the state's attorney's office is up and running, they seem to have a more equal marriage, a better sense of partnership: they talk about their day and conflicts in the office, as well as their lives with the kids. Even Owen guesses that Alicia is ghostwriting some of Peter's effective political speeches, and influencing his policy positions. And yet she says nothing at all to Caitlin about any of this.

Who's Your Daddy?

Simply thinking about who parents in *The Good Wife* demonstrates the ways in which the show both presents and minimizes work-family conflicts as women's only. Other than Alicia, there are simply no other regular female cast members who combine family life with career. Diane Lockhart and Kalinda Sharma are childless; the women we see working for the state's attorney, as far as we can tell, are all young and single. Frequent Lockhart Gardner opponent Patti Nyholm is regularly seen with her infant, but entirely as a strategic or tactical move: she uses her pregnancy and motherhood, variously, to get pity from judges, as a decoy or stalling tactic, or to get leverage over somebody.

And the men of *The Good Wife* are essentially free from the obligations of children. Eli Gold's adult daughter periodically shows up onscreen, but this is entirely for comic relief; she deflates his arrogance, but needs no active parenting. The only other working father we see regularly is ace investigator Andrew Wiley, who never appears onscreen without being encumbered by an infant in a Baby Bjorn or a stroller. He too comes close to caricature; despite being perennially harassed by babies and toddlers, he manages to follow conversations, pose tricky lines of questions, and catch offhand remarks effortlessly. This rings false to those of us who've actually had to bring a child to work (always on the To Be Avoided list after the first attempt), where invariably a work conversation is accompanied by queries of "Mommy?" and concentration is always a challenge.

While Peter is an affectionate father, he's a minority-status parent. He's willing to leverage his state's attorney status when it's absolutely necessary. He appears at a middle of the day interview at a prep school, but only because he and Alicia want to keep closer tabs on Grace after a kidnapping scare ("What Went Wrong"). But his weekend-dad status is obvious; when Alicia must work an overnight for a mediation, Uncle Owen gets drafted for kid care instead of Father Peter ("Get a Room"). Alicia is visibly pleasantly surprised early in their separation, when Peter says that he can take the children to school on Monday after their weekend with him ("A New Day").

The fact that this pretty modest contribution from Peter pleases Alicia speaks to the endless double standard the culture holds towards working fathers; they are expected to do little, and then praised for whatever they can offer. Indeed, during the prep-school interview, when Alicia has to step into the hall for a call from work, the headmistress expresses surprise because usually husbands are the ones who need to leave school meetings for work. Alicia's sardonic grimace when Peter responds, "We take turns," speaks to the fact that she carries the burden of parenting on a daily basis.

The only male character who makes a vigorous defense of the need for working parents to have a viable home life is Louis Canning; when he offers Alicia a job, he makes a passionate appeal to Alicia that her hours will be shorter and more humane if she works for him, because he himself wants to be an active parent to his children ("Parenting Made Easy").

Moms Get. It. Done.

While the show in many ways suggests the domestic benefits of two working parents, it also hints at some ways in which a mom who works can actually be unexpectedly effective. We've seen news articles suggesting that women's greater caution about risk makes them better CEOs than men, as they are less likely to risk a company's future and reputation on risky credit default swaps. *The Good Wife* often has funny moments in which we see Alicia's mom skills being put to excellent and unexpected legal use. Early in Season One, she gets identified as someone who can take care of clients; she has a knack for keeping clients calm. While this might reasonably seem like lame gender essentialism, "Mommy knows when the client needs his pacifier," what we actually see onscreen is her ability to listen quietly and fully, something every good parent tries to do. She also comes across as caring and sincere. Alicia is often able to express empathy for her clients, to speak outside her technical legal expertise and honestly, in ways that make them connect with her ("Hi"). Her ability to listen and be empathic serves her firm well: Alicia's maternal instincts often save the day, and these instincts are not part of the law school curriculum.

Most comically, the show contrasts Alicia's quiet ability to listen to a client ("Infamy") with Cary Agos's assumption that caring for a client means lecturing him. In this same episode, when he is abruptly assigned to handhold a client Alicia has effortlessly helped, Cary visibly alienates and irritates the client (whose girl has been kidnapped from a grocery store, and whose wife has committed suicide after talk TV has accused her of murder) by nattering endlessly and pointlessly about his own experience with death.

We also see the reversal of this equation as well; Alicia's lawyer skills get put to use on the home front. Most obviously, Alicia's battle with Jackie over the Florrick house reveals this: Jackie's tools are emotional manipulation and tears (which Jackie displays quite subtly; "Pants on Fire" and "Dream Team"). Alicia's ultimate threat to Jackie that she will stop Jackie's purchase is a legal one; "I'm a lawyer—watch me" she says to Jackie ("Pants on Fire"), before announcing that she will sue Jackie unless Jackie puts the house in the kids' names ("Dream Team"). On a more prosaic level, Alicia's experience taking depositions, and paying attention to pauses and nuance, doubtless helps her pick up on Zach's discomfort after Peter tells him the real reason for the separation ("Death Zone").

And it's for moments like this that *The Good Wife* is so addictive. Because what every working parent knows is that ultimately, work life and family life aren't in balance—they're just life, and they influence each other even when you're not aware of it. Alicia Florrick shows us this. Even when the show takes the easy way out of debates about how we value work, and how work structures and expectations need to be more sustainable with a private life (for the child-free too, let's be clear), it still spends a ton of time showing the reality of the working parent, in its messiness and contradiction. Through it all, Alicia Florrick is a completely compelling character as a working parent; her competence and calmness in a stressful job don't undermine her ability to be a fully present and compassionate mom. And I haven't even started on how fabulous her wardrobe is.

VI

Virtues and Vices

13
The Virtue of a Politician's Spouse

JOHN R. FITZPATRICK

The first season of *The Good Wife* begins and ends with a pair of symmetrical bookends. As we are introduced to Alicia Florrick she holds the hand of her politician husband, Peter, who's announcing at a press conference his resignation from his position as head of the Cook County State's Attorney's Office.

Peter's been involved in a scandal with a high-priced call girl, and there are numerous questions, including whether this is a sign of the corrupt practices which would enable such an extravagant lifestyle for a salaried public servant. Alicia's there to support her husband. If Alicia is still willing to support Peter, then perhaps the potential jury pool should as well.

This strategy fails, as Peter is eventually convicted on charges of corruption, and sent to state prison. He appeals this conviction, is granted a new trial, and is eventually vindicated. The first season of this series revolves around how Alicia, the namesake good wife, adapts to the changing circumstances following from Peter's legal problems.

After Peter is freed he decides to run in an election to regain his old job. The final episode of the first season ends with Peter announcing his candidacy at another press conference where Alicia is expected to stand by her man. Once again, if Alicia is willing to forgive Peter, apparently the voters of Chicagoland should do so as well. But as Peter holds out his hand, Alicia hesitates. This is the cliffhanger that sets up the second season.

Should the Voters Care About Alicia?

This is a complicated question. In the political universe of *The Good Wife* the politicians believe so. It also seems that in this fictional universe people do care about this. Peter's campaign manager Eli Gold is constantly after Alicia to help with Peter's image. And this seems to mirror the scrutiny that spouses of recent presidential candidates have undergone. An example in our recent presidential campaign was the vitriolic response to the remark by political commentator Hilary Rosen that Mitt Romney's wife "had never worked a day in her life." This led to another round of the "mommy wars"—should Hillary Clinton have stayed home and baked cookies?

We could respond that the political campaign in *The Good Wife* is highly artificial. There is too much character talk and not enough issues talk. Maybe Ann Romney is a rich spoiled princess and maybe this says something about Mitt, but isn't this election about political economy? Even if I think Mitt is a complete phony and not a guy I would want to have a beer with, there is a compelling argument that if Romney's announced policies seem preferable to those supplied by Barack Obama's record then I should hold my nose and give Romney my vote no matter what I believe about Mitt's character. Politicians don't always implement the policies they run on, (such as Obama on Guantanamo Bay, or George H.W. Bush's famous "no new taxes"), but they often do to a large extent (like Obama with healthcare and Iraq, and George W. Bush with tax cuts.)

Right Actions

Most of the modern ethical approaches concern right action, and the fundamental question is: What is the right thing to do? Thus, ethical theories that follow from this approach are primarily about right conduct and obligation. So, some examples:

Ethical Egoism: Morality requires us to perform those actions that are in our own rational self-interest. Eli offers many instances of egoistic conduct. He seems to be willing in Season Two to do almost anything to help Peter win, and thus advance his own career. In Season Three, he throws his ex-wife under the proverbial bus and after doing so gets the Democratic Party's blessing for Peter's campaign.

Consequentialism: Morality requires us to perform those actions that will produce the best consequences when the interests of all relevant parties are considered. Early in Season One, Alicia has a tough case where her first pro bono client is facing a retrial for murder. When she discusses the case with Peter in prison, it's clear that she and her client need help. Peter decides that in this case the ends justify the means. Even though this violates the rules of the state's attorney's office, an oath that he has an obligation to obey and maintain even after resigning, Peter tells her there may have been "pitted" evidence in this case; evidence the police did not disclose in discovery. We might be concerned that Alicia is violating her own client's confidentiality, but in the context of the episode it's clear that Peter is well aware of the details of the case. Alicia cannot divulge what Peter already knows.

Deontology: Morality requires us to follow rules of conduct that conform to duty, obligations and rights. In the above example of consequentialism, Peter violated the confidentiality of his former office for the greater good, but Alicia can be seen on many occasions to refuse to follow his lead. For example, when Alicia defends Jonas Stern on a DUI she learns that he was not intoxicated; he has a form of dementia. But having learned this while functioning as his attorney Alicia feels compelled to keep his secret even when this knowledge would be useful for the firm. Obviously, if Jonas' condition were to become public, this would be problematic for the firm; his cases could become subject to re-litigation. However, the private internal use of this information would be valuable to Will and Diane. But Jonas insists that she not disclose it, and she honors her duty.

Social Contract Theory: Morality requires us to follow rules of conduct that rational, self-interested people would agree are fair and mutually beneficial. I will agree not to do harmful or unfair things to you if you will make the same agreement with me. The almost classic illustration is when the Florrick and Childs campaigns agree to leave the other's children alone and outside the campaign.

In all these cases we are justifying moral conduct through the process of evaluating the morality of their *actions*, and we morally evaluate people based on their performing or avoiding those actions that the theory either requires or forbids.

Virtuous People

The ethics of virtue, on the other hand, begins with a different fundamental question: What traits of character make one a good person? Another way to put it is: What is it to be a virtuous person? In this case the question is not right conduct but rather right disposition, mental and emotional composure, or *character*—not whether one performs the right actions but rather whether one has the right virtues. Thus, under this approach, we should be more interested in character rather than conduct. We are less interested in what a person does, and more interested in whether he or she is virtuous.

What are virtues? Standardly, virtues are traits of character that when properly habituated allow one to live well. Thus, an honest person is one who through a process of habituation has developed the character trait of being truthful as a matter of course, of being forthright and reliable in their claims, rather than one who engages in dissembling, equivocation, obfuscation and other more mundane forms of lying.

There are many virtues and virtue theorists often choose a few or many, but we'd expect to find these traits in a virtuous person: benevolence, civility, compassion, cleanliness, courage, fairness, generosity, gratitude, honesty, industry, justice, loyalty, moderation, non-malevolence, optimism, patience, prudence, reasonableness, self-control, tactfulness, and tolerance.

The Good Wife raises issues about virtue theory. What character traits make a person a good lawyer? All our attorneys are hard working, well prepared, have great powers of concentration, and show courage under fire. But they each have personal strengths based on their individual characters. Diane Lockhart is great at pre-trial motions. Will Gardner is great at creating reasonable doubt. Cary Argos is great at making the guilty look guilty. And Alicia excels in nurturing clients through the system. It seems their individual characters allow them to excel in their given fields.

We can go all the way back to Aristotle in his famous *Nicomachean Ethics* where he argues that the virtues are traits of character that allow one to "live well" or be "happy" (the Greek word, *eudaimonia*, is what he used). *Eudaimonia* is not concerned with *basic* pleasures (like for sex, food, and the like) and if there is pleasure involved, it's more like joy or satisfaction at being virtuous and doing what's right. For example, Alicia's life as a working mom gives her great satisfaction, but not a great deal of pleasure; she has a life of great joy, but not one of great fun. *Eudaimonia* has been translated as "successful" too, and this works well so long as we don't merely mean financial or political (fortune or fame) success; rather, it's more like the success of having lived a virtuous and good life worthy of praise. Cary is far more successful as a prosecutor than as a defense attorney, but he makes less money.

Practical Activity and Contemplation

And this leads us to a question that is at least as old as Western philosophy itself is: what's the good life and how is one to live it? In Book One of the *Nicomachean Ethics*, Aristotle appears to suggest that the best life is one that is devoted to practical activities and virtues like those associated with civility, courage, fairness, generosity, honesty, justice, prudence, reasonableness, and tactfulness. In Book Ten, however, he recommends the life of philosophic contemplation with corresponding intellectual virtues as the best way to live. This life of contemplation would include not only basic book smarts type of stuff one learns about in a standard school curriculum (math, science, history, politics, and the like), but also being able to offer explanations for the workings of things in reality, as well as knowledge of basic logic and argumentation (Aristotle actually invented a branch of logic known as *categorical logic*).

Clearly, Aristotle doesn't think we should *only* be sitting around like philosophers contemplating and debating things. Life as a citizen seems to entail more practical activity than is necessary for mere survival. In ancient Athens, just as in modern Chicagoland, bills must be paid, children must be raised, and garbage must be collected, and if this makes little sense for the average citizen, it makes less for a politician. One possible resolution is to limit our practical activities to the minimum necessary for the life of contemplation. But it doesn't seem likely that Aristotle would offer such an odd and counter-intuitive candidate for the good life. A more plausible attempt to resolve the dichotomy is to realize that any activity can be overdone—whatever is the most pleasurable activity would eventually become unpleasant from its overuse.

Although there are many interpretations, it would seem that both of these activities are essential parts of what make human existence a complete and flourishing life of self-actualization (to use Maslow's term). And politicians and lawyers need both probably even more so than the rest of us, given their social responsibilities. To be a great governor, Peter would need a philosophical vision, and have the practical wisdom that allows him to get things done.

A Tapestry of Activities

Aristotle is no dummy, and he recognized the importance of both practical activity and philosophical contemplation in his construction of the good life. What's still an open question is whether one activity is the dominant one to be supported by the other.

In Book One of the *Nicomachean Ethics*, Aristotle claims that to find the good of a thing we have to find what function it serves. This function is just not any activity that a thing performs but that special activity that it does not share; the exclusive activity that in a sense defines it. Thus, the function of a claw hammer is to drive in and pull out nails. The function of a ballpeen hammer is to shape metal. The function of a lawyer will be to advocate for a client well. The purpose of a governor is to govern well. For Aristotle, the function of a human being will be an activity of the soul that is in accord with reason.

In his Book Seven account of pleasure, he suggests that the life of *eudaimonia* is pleasant and that we should "weave pleasure into happiness." The point Aristotle's making here is that it's simply not coherent to talk of separating the pleasant aspect of the good life from the good life as a whole. Activities that are unpleasant are difficult to engage in; they are impeded. Philosophic contemplation, as has already been stated, is hard work. It needs a certain environment to flourish. The pleasure that comes to us in philosophic contemplation is an essential component of it. There is no possibility of philosophic contemplation while the inquisitor crushes your bones.

More importantly, Aristotle wants the good life to be pleasant. The good life is a complete life; if the good life lacked pleasure it would be impeded and thus not complete. The model we get of the good life here is one of a tapestry that pleasure is woven through. The good life is the interweaving of the activities that it is composed of. This model of the good life, a tapestry of interwoven activities, can also be found in Aristotle's Book Nine account of the importance of friendship.

Good Friends and the Good Life

In Book One Aristotle states that the self-sufficient life is not the solitary one. In Book Nine he elaborates on this in some detail. The important point here is that Aristotle clearly argues that the kind of contemplation the virtuous person will wish to engage in is dependent on his or her having good friends. If, as Aristotle suggests, we can "contemplate our neighbors better than ourselves" and judge their characters better than our own, then we are better able to form better characters and perform more noble actions if we surround ourselves with virtuous friends. One theme that runs across various plotlines in *The Good Wife* is the notion of mentorship. Will, Diane, Derrick Bell, and David Lee serve at various times as mentors to Alicia, and as the series evolves we see Alicia begin to mentor others as well. Mentors are valuable since as Aristotle argues we can see the noble and virtuous actions better in others that try to reinvent the wheel on our own.

There is a continued interplay among many activities in Aristotle's conception of the good life. The source of much of what we will wish to contemplate will come from our friends. What will help motivate us in this regard is that it's pleasant to examine and contemplate the actions of virtue that we can find in good friends. But what's really striking here is that the worthy actions that are my own are also those of the good person who is my friend. Aristotle must be rejecting here any notion of philosophic contemplation as a solitary activity. Philosophic contemplation must be an activity that individuals engage in together. Friendship in a philosophic community is essential for philosophic contemplation "for by oneself it is not easy to be continuously active; but with others and toward others it is easier."

A solitary life inhibits the life of philosophic contemplation and the communal life motivates it. When Aristotle states that activities with others and toward others are easier, we can take him to mean that even for a philosopher of his magnitude he finds himself more motivated and productive when working in a group. And Lockhart Gardner is more than the sum of its parts. But if we become good people by surrounding ourselves with good people, and we need role models to inform us, and friends to motivate us, then suddenly there seem to be reasons to ask who are the people in Peter's life.

Once we realize that philosophy does not exist in a vacuum we have come full circle. If we need the company of others, colleagues of good will and virtue, to engage in philosophic contemplation with, then clearly we need a polis (a community) in which to find them. But if we need a polis then we need practical activity to maintain it.

So for Aristotle the best life seems to one that weaves pleasure, friendship, and practical activity into a coherent whole. And if this is the case, when we assess a politician or anyone else for that matter, the assessment will be most complete when we ask questions about how that coherent whole hangs together.

Alicia Matters

But if people are only as good as the virtuous friends they surround themselves, then perhaps this is a legitimate way to assess the virtue of a politician. Politicians are often very skilled at presenting a public persona at odds with their individual temperament. If so, we might get behind the curtain by looking at their friends including their spouse.

We want politicians that have good character traits. What then become the criteria that we should use for evidence of a politician's character, and are the character traits of the politician's spouse relevant?

In both real life and *The Good Wife*, there seems to be little correlation between the effectiveness of politicians in office and the quality of their marriage. In the first three seasons, as Peter and Alicia's marriage crashes, Peter seems to have become a less corrupt politician, and Alicia has developed into a better person. But the character traits of a spouse may help reveal a more complete narrative of the candidate's life. And to the extent that this narrative is important, the spouse is important.

The ironic point of the third season is that Alicia's support of Peter's run for governor does make a real difference in assessing Peter's character. But it's Alicia the good *person* whose support is convincing, not Alicia the good wife. Peter lacks the traits that make someone a good spouse, but he may well have the makings of a great governor. And Alicia is perfectly situated to see this. So, when all is said and done, her endorsement matters.

14
Alicia Saint
of Professionals

Ana Carolina Azevedo and
Marco Antonio Azevedo

Alicia Florrick spent fifteen years of her life as a happy housewife and just didn't see it coming. When her husband pulled the rug out from under her feet with nothing less than a sex scandal, she had no option but to go back to work and keep her personal affairs from mingling with her public image. In spite of the difficulties surrounding her new life, she always goes out of her way to deliver a job of professional excellence.

Whether her clients are innocent underdogs or guilty-looking bigots, Alicia defends them equally. She always comes off as the better person, having been nicknamed "Saint Alicia" by those who recognize her distinctiveness compared with other lawyer characters who have different morals and, sometimes, make her feel like hers are too high for the job.

Lawyers act on behalf of their clients; but as members of the legal profession they are also officers of the legal system and public citizens who have a special responsibility to bring about justice. There's a lot of bureaucracy involved in such a status—you don't just get up and become a lawyer. You have to graduate with a certain GPA, take an oath and pass the bar exam, and only then can you represent someone in a lawsuit, thus consolidating the ultimate link between you and your profession. Lawyers are supposed to be paradigmatic examples of *professionals*, meaning that they abide by a set of ethically based, pragmatic rules conventionally designated by a group of workers to guide their whole clan as to the way they lead their work life.

Plato and Professions

The ethics and pragmatics of professions goes all the way back to Plato (429–347 B.C.E.) and his discussion in his most famous work, *Republic*. In Book I, Plato has Socrates in a dialogue with the sophist Thrasymachus and Socrates argues that a politician rules not for his own interest but for the best interests of the governed.

Socrates draws an analogy between politics and medicine. Assuming that medicine doesn't consider the interest of the doctor, but rather the "interest of the body," he reaches the conclusion that its best interest is not towards the practitioner, but the patient. Hence, a professional practitioner is good not because she's got money, glory, or personal success, but because of the good provided to those by her practice: the patient, the client, and, in the case of politics, the citizen.

Thrasymachus is the practical realist in the dialogue—so to speak—and doesn't agree with this. People do things mainly to please themselves rather than acting through altruistic motives. Therefore, how could professionals care more about their clients than the other way around? Thrasymachus goes on then to say that if one could live unjustly without any burdens, one would be happier than the just. That is, if you had to choose between the grueling rewards of a life of integrity and that of a goldbrick benefited by treachery, you would be tempted to choose the latter.

As you can figure, this seems to imply a certain lack of virtue. But Thrasymachus's point is that this is exactly what we should recognize, if we don't want to be hypocrites. People aren't honest, or other-centered, or naturally just toward each other—they just want to look like they are, so others won't hold anything against them. And they sure as heck aren't particularly interested in being virtuous, since virtue is only useful in the presence of others, and what most matters in life is glory and power.

Alicia and Eli

Even the best legal mind requires the Socratic method to keep itself sharp.

—ALICIA TO STERN, "Threesome," Season One

"Saint" Alicia and Eli represent two different views and moral ideologies about what really matters in life. Alicia clearly represents the Socratic view, the view that virtue and integrity are non-negotiable values. She's the kind of professional who always has the best interest of her clients and her own profession in mind. This is a distinct moral attitude. At its core is the moral idea that if we really care about what happens to others, we can't worry solely about our own pleasure and enjoyment. What we *are* is not equivalent to what we *appear* to be, nor is personal well-being the same as the total amount of pleasure and enjoyment we can attain in the course of our lives.

Eli, on the other hand, leans toward Thrasymachus's view, taking personal glory as the main target of his efforts. Eli illustrates his opposite opinion in the Season Four episode, "Don't Haze Me, Bro" when he notes: "I lie for a living." His cunning, lying, and making up excuses for bad behavior are contrary to Alicia's personal choice for truth, and probably why she likes to keep a distance from him.

Nevertheless, Eli may be the way he is because it's his job to give good advice in order for his clients to succeed, just like a lawyer's job. So, there seems to be a link between Alicia and Eli, since lawyers also fight on behalf of their clients' interests. All lawyers want to win their cases—and note that, in adjudications, this implies that another party has to lose. In this case, Alicia and Eli's professionalism wouldn't be so different after all. If Thrasymachus is right, Alicia is merely being naive and foolish when she resists employing whatever means she has for winning her cases.

Professionalism versus Consultation

DERRICK: There is someone else you can blame.
ALICIA: Who?
DERRICK: The victims. Do you have a problem with that?
ALICIA: Do you mean as a lawyer or as a person?

—Season Two, "Cleaning House"

We know that professionals abide by a certain set of rules, and Plato helped us to see that professionals have the best interest of their clients in mind. Sociologist Eliot Freidson adds to the description of professionalism, noting that to be a professional is to be part of a group of experts in a certain area or field of study. Attorneys and physicians can be cited as paradigmatic examples of professionals.

Following this characterization, Alicia is a professional—Kalinda, and probably Eli, are not. This isn't because they have different "moral" characters. The point is that the natures of their roles are different; unsurprisingly, their character traits express different and contrasting occupational virtues. If Freidson's right, Kalinda, for example, would likely behave differently if she was a lawyer and not an investigator.

Thanks goodness we don't live in a world without the sort of professionalism that Freidson suggests because, if we did, we'd probably be at risk all the time. You don't call a plumber to handle your legal case? So too, you don't hire a lawyer to handle your plumbing problems. Also, without someone to take the stand for us, we would feel incredibly naked in the world, because we can't be good at everything. Imagine how much time we'd spend acquiring enough knowledge to be our own lawyers, physicians, or even plumbers. That's a good reason why Alicia's clients ask her for guidance so much.

Not all consulting occupations are professional occupations; it's possible to be a consultant and not a professional in the way we've talked about them so far. Eli is a consulting expert and a campaign manager, but he doesn't fit the label of professional like Will and Alicia do. Why not? Although he may an expert, he's not really a member of a group committed to the interests of a profession, and it's surely questionable whether he has any moral code by which to perform his work.

Eli doesn't stick by his convictions in the Season Three episode, "The Penalty Box," when he chooses not to consult on his ex-wife's campaign after the Democratic Party threatens to stop supporting Peter if he does. But it's ultimately Eli's choice to make (otherwise they wouldn't be threatening him), and he balances his interests with caution, choosing at last to stay with Peter's campaign, his longest commitment. If Eli had as much as a fight with Peter, he might've sent the Democrats back where they belonged, and that wouldn't keep him from working in his field again because of the nature of his occupation. In other words, Eli doesn't give a damn because he owes nothing to anybody in particular. His client's glory is his own, and to heck with any set of principled regulations.

What do you think happens to Eli, the image consultant, or Kalinda, the private investigator, when they screw up? They might become infamous, but nobody's going stop them from keeping their practice. But as far as lawyers are concerned, when you do get caught with your hands in the cookie jar, you don't just owe a few apologies or get to be all Eli Gold–like blasé about it: naughty lawyers who disgrace the oath deserve to be sanctioned. Or at least it should be like that, for the sake of the profession's moral integrity. People of low virtue represent a danger to their own professions. Professionals have privileges outsiders don't, giving them something of a monopoly over their field. Crooks within professions are serious perils to their clients and to the general public.

Welcome to the Dark Side

ALICIA: I just, for one minute, wanted to think that we were doing the right thing.

WILL: But we are doing the right thing.

ALICIA: But for the wrong reason.

WILL: Who do you know is doing something for the right reason? I would love to meet them, because my guess is, after five minutes of questioning, we'll find the wrong reason.

—"Great Firewall," Season Two

Some professionals in *The Good Wife* do manage to avoid the detection of their wrongful exploits. In the course of her work life, Alicia meets some very contrasting personas. These are people who bring new issues to the table by dazzling and convincing jurors and judge by means of stunts that transcend legal proficiency. Alicia may wear her heart on her sleeve when she's working, but her opponents usually keep trickier stuff up theirs.

For example, the cute, fair-skinned, blonde Nancy Crozier knows exactly how her looks affect the way people treat her. The law should be blind, so as to base judgments on argumentation only, but this one knows how the cookie actually crumbles, so she abuses visual aids to hypnotize the judges. Crozier seems to know that to influence others you have to act empathetic towards them (then again, you don't have to actually be what you're appearing to be). She uses statements in court to bring up sensitive topics she thinks most judges will likely agree to or identify with and utilizes counterfeit ingenuousness to suggest honesty—so, she asks jurors if they'll feel uncomfortable during a trial "mostly about sex," employs innocent, childish words instead of adult ones to refer to sex, or twitches when she's talking about it in Season Two's "Getting Off." That's pure manipulation, which seems nothing like professionalism.

Also consider Patti Nyholm. When her client's about to give himself away while being questioned by Alicia, the pregnant Patti stops her client just in time claiming she's feeling contractions ("Getting Off"). Clutching her enormous belly, she decides it's time to call off the meeting, right in the middle of it. Women have been demanding equality at work for a long time, and the last thing you should do if you support the cause is to play dirty using a women-only weapon. Alicia feels frustrated to have to share a profession and gender with such a person, because Patti is ruining her reputation both as a lawyer and a working woman and mother.

Crozier and Nyholm use feminine traits to aid them in court, but Louis Canning found his own device for winning the jurors' hearts. He even uses his tardive dyskinesia symptoms to bring the spotlight back to him when it's the other lawyer's turn to cross-examine. His unorthodox methods to win trials include helping Alicia when she's in distress, just to get close enough to her information, and even taking things from her briefcase ("Parenting Made Easy").

There are other cases of questionable professional lawyering. Will Gardner is a player—with the ladies, in the courtroom and on the court with a basketball. He plays around with girls and practically toys with his profession as he strives to make the firm ascend. He's not portrayed as a manipulative or immoral person like the aforementioned lawyers, but he's faced accusations regarding his relationship with judges outside of the courtrooms, not to mention his suspension for taking money from a client to pay off his own debts.

Jonas Stern, one of the firm's partners, hires Alicia in order to represent him against a DUI charge. After some investigating, she finds out that Stern is suffering from early signs of dementia. Alicia urges him to come clean about it, but he promptly refuses, as he couldn't bear leaving his practice and smearing his reputation with a disease, and demands that she finds another way to get him exonerated without disclosing his sad secret.

What's wrong with all those lawyers? Do they not take the law seriously? Their ways make us wonder if they go through the same dilemmas we know Alicia does because she's uttered them to Cary Agos over a bar counter in "The Penalty Box" (Season Three). What could it be that keeps Alicia from going completely cuckoo around these people?

Alicia's Virtue Professionalism

The answer can be found through Plato's student, Aristotle (384–322 B.C.E.). Several philosophers, aided by Aristotle's view, see virtue as a good habit whereby we cultivate a kind of balance in our character. The idea is to promote the "not too much" or "not too little," but the "just right" in our characters so that our actions and reactions to situations reflect this hitting of the mean between two extremes.

The virtuous person has cultivated the kind of character whereby she knows how to act and react in the right way, at the right time, in the right manner, and for the right reasons in each and every moral dilemma encountered. However, the way in which you cultivate a virtuous character is through choosing actions that are conducive to building that virtuous character. For example, if you want to cultivate the virtue of honesty so that you can actually be an honest person, then you need to act honestly time and time again so that the virtue can "sink in" to your character. The more Johnny actually tells the truth when asked whether he has done something wrong, the more Johnny cultivates the virtue of honesty. The more Suzy lies when asked whether she has done something wrong, the more she cultivates the vice of dishonesty.

Aristotle's position is somewhat unique in that it places emphasis on the disposition or character from which the moral action stems—as opposed to focusing on the principles behind, or consequences of, an action. Because the concern is to promote a good or virtuous character, this moral position is known as *virtue ethics*. The virtue ethicists' central idea is that if you have a virtuous character, then not only will you likely perform morally right actions, but also these actions likely will have good consequences. We want to not only perform right actions that have good consequences, we also want to be *virtuous persons* performing right actions that have good consequences. You can get Crozier, Nyholm, Garner, or Stern to do the right thing yielding good consequences; however, they're probably still a bit vicious and scumbaggy.

Virtue ethicists have a general list of virtues, including honesty, courage, prudence, generosity, integrity, affability, and respect, to name just a few. Professionalism is the key virtue for our purposes here, and it can be viewed as a cluster of virtues attached to a specific and specifiable sort of role-behavior. Aristotle actually argued that the virtues we get by exercising those traits "also happens in the case of professions as well." Since Alicia promotes right acts associated with her profession and her clients in the right manner, in the right place, and at the right time consistently throughout the show, she's a great example of someone who has cultivated the virtue of professionalism. She's not a typical bottom-feeder lawyer—like the stereotypes of Crozier, Nyholm, Garner, or Stern—she seems to be a good person, a good wife, and a good lawyer.

Being Good All of the Time?

So, we've seen that professionals not only abide by a certain set of rules and have the best interest of their clients in mind (Plato), but they also are part of a group of experts in a certain area or field of study (Friedson), and they're not merely consultants. Above all, they should be good, virtuous persons, as Aristotle emphasizes.

Being good all the time exonerates you from feeling guilty or pressured by society, but it adds too much pressure as well. Maybe the good wife doesn't want to be overwhelmed with the responsibilities of being a good mother, wife, daughter-in-law, attorney, and person. Maybe she wants out. Well, one way out is to choose the reward that will take the pressure off her shoulders for the time being. She gives in to temptation and is not perfect, despite being the good wife. Even Aristotle recognizes, however, that not every virtuous person can be good *all* of the time.

Three years have passed since Alicia Florrick joined Lockhart Gardner. Now, she's got a heap of cases piled up on her resume and the series suggest there are more to come. Perhaps she's reached the point just before no return from the life of a good wife. What's next: turning into a shark at last, or going back to integrity?

But as Alicia and we all know, we may make some mistakes along our journey, but they won't count as much as our striving for virtue.

Women Lawyers—Good, Bad, and Memorable

Alicia Florrick, Diane Lockhart, Caitlin D'arcy, Geneva Pine, Dana Lodge, and Elsbeth Tascioni—all female lawyers in *The Good Wife*. As a salute to female lawyers in the real world, we offer the following:

The Good . . .

BETTISIA GOZZADINI (1209–1261) supposedly not only got an education disguised as a man, but also taught from behind a curtain when she lectured in law at the University of Bologna. She may have been the first woman to obtain a position at a university.

The first female lawyer in American history was ARABELLA MANSFIELD (1846–1911). She was able to take the Iowa state bar exam in early 1869, and received high marks, even though at the time only white men over the age of twenty-one could legally practice law. Near the end of 1869 Iowa changed the law concerning attorneys, allowing women and minorities to practice law; however, although Mansfield had the option of practicing law in Iowa, she chose the academic life, ultimately becoming the Dean of the School of Music at Depauw University in Greencastle, Indiana.

MYRA BRADWELL (1831–1894) passed the Illinois bar exam in 1869, but was prevented from practicing law because she was a woman. The case went all the way to the US Supreme Court and in *Bradwell v. Illinois* (83 U.S. 16 Wall. 130, 1873) Justice Joseph Bradley wrote the oft-quoted:

The natural and proper timidity and delicacy which belongs to the female sex evidently unfits it for many of the occupations of civil life . . . The paramount destiny and mission of a woman are to fulfill the noble and benign offices of wife and mother. This is the law of the Creator.

However, in 1892 Bradwell ended up receiving her license to practice law in Illinois due to an 1873 Illinois Supreme Court ruling that made it illegal to exclude anyone from doing lawyerly work "on account of gender."

CHARLOTTE E. RAY (1850–1911) was the first black woman admitted to the bar in the United States (1872) and the first female lawyer to practice in Washington, DC. There's a story that she used the name "C.E. Ray" when she applied to Howard University's School of Law—the idea being that no one would know she was a woman or black—but this is likely not true since Howard was known for its acceptance of women and minorities at the time.

GLORIA ALLRED (b. 1941) is a famous American lawyer who is known for representing celebrities, advocating the protection of women's rights, and utilizing the media to her advantage. She gained national exposure in 1987 when she sued the Friar's Club of Beverly Hills, California over its all-male admission policy and won, effectively becoming the first female member in its then forty-year history.

"Having family responsibilities and concerns just has to make you a more understanding person." No doubt the writers of *The Good Wife* would agree with this quotation from SANDRA DAY O'CONNOR (b. 1930), who was appointed the first female Supreme Court Justice of the US in 1981. She served twenty-five years on the Court and developed a reputation for being centrist, pragmatic, and willing to make judgments on a case-by-case basis.

. . . The Bad . . .

"Her felony conviction would not necessarily prevent her from practicing law in Virginia," so reported the *Richmond Times Dispatch* in a story about JENNIFER MARIE PATTERSON, who graduated from the University of Richmond School of Law in January, 2011, and was sentenced in the fall of 2011 to three years in prison for selling methamphetamine from 2007 to 2009. Apparently, she was selling it to support her own habit, citing the fast-paced, intense environment of law school as the reason for her addiction. Her own lawyer did note, however, that she stopped using cocaine in 2008, meth in 2009, marijuana in 2010, and alcohol in 2011. Good for her!

In the fall of 2012, a Missouri attorney specializing in estate planning named SUSAN VAN NOTE was accused of shooting her father and his longtime girlfriend back in 2010. The girlfriend died immediately, but the old man survived for a few more days in a hospital where Van Note was by his side while police searched for the shooter(s). But that's not all—Van Note apparently forged a document making her durable power of attorney for her dad, as well as forged a "Do not resuscitate" document, allowing her father to die from the gunshot she caused. Now *that's* bad.

Nigerian lawyer ADENIKE OSIJOLA was charged with damage to property, house breaking, unlawful assembly, breach of public peace, conspiracy, and impersonation in 2010 after she was arrested for stealing $64,000.00 worth of valuables from a small company in the port city of Lagos, Nigeria.

Fighting, drinking, embezzling, perjuring, cheating on one's spouse, running a brothel, and, of course, murder—these are all activities that came to light at the various trials concerning attorney MARY LEONARD (1845–1912). The thing is, she was the accused each time! Leonard was the first female lawyer admitted to the bar in Oregon in 1886, and studied law after being acquitted of her husband's murder. In one of her other trials (1897) where she was accused of threatening to kill the landlord of her (ahem) boarding house, she admitted to carrying around a gun and a hammer for protection. Quite the hell raiser for a woman at her time.

. . . And the Memorable

In 1945–1946 the Allies held trials in Nuremburg, Germany, to prosecute Nazi war criminals, and American lawyers MARY KAUFFMAN and CECELIA GOETZ were able to secure spots on the prosecution team. The male lawyers on the team looked on Kauffman and Goetz with scorn, making them sign a waiver of disability due to their "female condition."

CONSTANCE BAKER MOTLEY (1921–2005) is memorable because not only was she the first black female federal judge (appointed by

President Lyndon Baines Johnson in 1966 to the Southern District Court of New York), but she also changed professional sports history in 1978 when she ruled that a woman reporter could be allowed in the New York Yankees' locker room.

In 1994 **RUTH BADER GINSBURG** (b. 1933) was appointed Associate Justice of the US Supreme Court by President Bill Clinton. She was one of nine women in a class of five hundred who entered Harvard Law School in 1956 and explained the low number of females this way:

> Why were there so few women in law school a generation ago? It was the sense that, well, I can go through three years of law school and then what? Who will hire me and how will I support myself? So many places were closed to women in those days. The most prestigious clerkships with judges were not open to women. Some of our most distinguished jurists simply refused to interview a female.

JAYASHREE SATPUTE (b. 1982) is a Delhi-based lawyer working in human rights. In 2010 a woman gave birth on the pavement in Delhi and then lay there for four days while hundreds of apathetic people stepped over her until she eventually died. Satpute used the case to convince the Delhi High Court to enact laws mandating that shelters for destitute pregnant women be set up so that no "destitute woman is compelled to give birth to a child on the footpath."

Philosophers Who Were Also Lawyers

Thrasymachus (around 459–400 b.c.e.)

At one point or another, every student of philosophy reads Plato's dialogue *Republic*, where Socrates and a few younger guys try to define justice.

In Book I of the *Republic* Socrates matches wits with a sophist named Thrasymachus who argues that injustice is "stronger, freer, and more masterful" than justice primarily because injustice is "what profits a man's self and is for his advantage." Socrates tries to get Thrasymachus to see that acting unjustly actually isn't to your advantage because it leads to a disordered, paranoid, pathological personality—basically, people will recognize that you're an unjust jerk and they'll either shun you or try to take you down. Thrasymachus taught budding politicians and noblemen in Athens how to use rhetoric to win arguments in law courts and citizen assemblies, and a good many sophists themselves were lawyers, too.

Sophists usually get a bad rap primarily because philosophers like Plato and Aristotle characterized them as money-grubbing, self-serving, truth-twisting jerks lacking in moral fiber. Maybe it does makes sense, then, that they were lawyers, huh?

Protagoras (around 490–420 b.c.e.)

This sophist is famous for having said, "Man is the measure of all things" implying that what is true or false, right or wrong, or even up or down is wholly dependent upon a person's perspective. And further, there are as many different perspectives about reality as there are different persons. You might say he was one of the first relativists.

Protagoras was also famous because, of all the sophists alive during his time, he supposedly charged the most money for his rhetorical teaching services. It's easy to see how getting a jury to believe that "it's all a matter of perspective" could help you win your case—provided, of course, that you can convince them to buy *your* perspective. Plato and Aristotle portray Protagoras in a negative light (you can tell they both friggin' hated him) with Aristotle claiming that he had a knack for "making the weaker argument appear stronger."

Demosthenes (384–322 b.c.e.)

This fellow could be considered the Godfather of Oration in the Western world. He was a lawyer, statesman, speechwriter, and a bit of a philosopher in Athens, being revered by other well-known orators such as Plutarch, Quintillian, and Cicero.

From about 357 B.C.E., Philip of Macedonia and the Macedonians were formally at war with Athens, and Demosthenes took it upon himself to be Philip's biggest opponent, regularly pontificating about the king being a menace, monster, and tyrant. This didn't go over very well, obviously, and although Philip's son, Alexander the Great, never got the chance to execute Demosthenes, his successor, Antipater, almost did. We say *almost* because Demosthenes poisoned himself before he could be captured by Antipater. The Liechtenstein Museum in Vienna, Austria has the Herm of Demosthenes, a stone sculpture with the head of Demosthenes and a vertically oriented rectangular torso on which can be found a stone version of Demosthenes' genitalia. That's all there is to it—head, rectangle, and his junk. And apparently it was really, really, really, really cold the day the sculpture was made.

Cicero (106-43 b.c.e.)

Not only is this the name of the Chicago suburb where Rob Arp grew up in the 1970s and 1980s, but this is also the name of one of the most important philosopher-lawyers in Western history. Actually, his full name is Marcus Tullius Cicero and many writers throughout history have referred to him (somewhat affectionately, at times) as "Tully."

"Tully" was a Roman statesman living during the reign of Julius Caesar and, after JC's assassination on the Ides of March in 44 B.C.E., he and Mark Antony became the biggest political hotshots in ancient Rome. However, Cicero disliked Antony, and over the course of a year wrote fourteen speeches attacking Antony called the *Philippics* hoping to oust the Big MA from power. This backfired, however, and Antony had Cicero's head and hands cut off and nailed to the rostra in the Roman Forum for all to see.

Robert Radford has noted that Cicero is a "sterling example of the rare combination of political power and philosophical wisdom in a single person." It may be that Cicero was the closest thing to a Philosopher King any society has every seen. However, Cicero did famously state that, "to study philosophy is nothing but to prepare one's self to die."

Lucius Mestrius Plutarchus, a.k.a. Plutarch (46–120)

Plutarch was a Greek philosopher, priest at Delphi, magistrate in Chaeronea, and historian who wrote *The Lives of the Roman Emperors from Augustus to Vitellius* and a clever piece titled, *Parallel Lives*, which consists of biographies of famous Greeks and Romans—including Julius Caesar, Alexander the Great, Mark Antony, and Cicero—that are laid out in "parallel" to show common traits of virtues as well as vices.

Choice quotations about virtue and vice from Plutarch include: "Character is long-standing habit," "A few vices are sufficient to darken many virtues," and "Courage consists not in hazarding without fear; but being resolutely minded in a just cause." Although, this one's pretty clever: "I don't need a friend who changes when I change and who nods when I nod; my shadow does that much better."

Ibn Rushd, a.k.a. Averroes (1126–1198)

Averroes was a Muslim philosopher who contributed greatly to the revival of Aristotle's philosophy in the West, specifically with his *Commentary on Aristotle's Metaphysics*. He wrote philosophy in his spare time, actually, as his primary job was as a jurist in Cordova, Spain. His grandfather, Abdul-Walid Muhammad, and his father, Abdul-Qasim Ahmad, both held the position of Chief Judge of Cordova.

Not only was Averroes an accomplished lawyer and philosopher, he was also a doctor who wrote two works, *Kitab al-Kulyat fi al-Tibb* and *Kitab al-Taisir fi al-Mudawat wa al-Tadbir*, which would act as the main medical textbooks for Muslims, as well as Jews and Christians in medical schools until the early Enlightenment.

Francis Bacon (1561–1626)

Most people know this name from history class because it's synonymous with the roots of the scientific method. And, people wrongly attribute the saying, "Knowledge is power" to Bacon. Bacon never said this in writing, but Bacon's friend Thomas Hobbes said something similar in his work titled, *Elementorum philosophiae sectio prima De corpore*: "The end of knowledge is power."

It's true that Bacon made important strides in modern science and the philosophy of science; but he was also a popular English lawyer during his lifetime. In fact, he was part of the legal team that found Robert Devereux, Second Earl of Essex, guilty of treason after Devereux's failed *coup d'état* against the English throne. In a bizarre twist of fate, the guy who was pardoned by Devereux and became a professional executioner is the same guy who chopped Devereux's head off in the Tower of London—after three attempts.

Hugo Grotius (1583–1645)

Grotius was a jurist and philosopher known for his defense of the Christian God's laws as a basis for natural laws that, in turn, act as the basis for human laws in societies. "What God has shown to be His Will," claims Grotius, "that is law. This axiom points directly to the cause of law, and is rightly laid down as the primary principle."

So, murder is illegal in any society not merely because it's immoral through natural law, but ultimately because it's sinful through God's law as laid down in the Ten Commandments. Grotius also made important strides in the development of international law and morality, especially regarding war. In fact, basic principles of his *De iure belli ac pacis libri tres* (On the Law of War and Peace) are still taught and adhered to by Western societies today. Supposedly, Gustavus Adolphus—king of Sweden from 1611 to 1632—kept a copy of the Bible and Grotius's *De iure belli ac* under his pillow.

René Descartes (1596–1650)

Before he was "thinking, therefore being" Descartes actually received a law degree in 1616 from the University of Poitiers in France. He went straight into the military after that, then traveled a lot to places like Bohemia, Hungary, and Germany before settling down in Holland in 1628 where he remained mostly for the next twenty years.

Although everyone has heard of Descartes's "I think, therefore I am," almost no one knows that Descartes is the father of classical analytic geometry. We all learned about the Cartesian co-ordinate x-y system in algebra classes in grade school—well, *Cartesian* is the adjectival form of Descartes. Descartes invented the whole thing.

Descartes was known to be kind of a sickly person who spent a lot of time in bed—mostly to sleep until 11:00 A.M. daily, but a lot of the time because he was actually ill. (In fact, Descartes died of pneumonia way too young supposedly because for a year he would get up at 5:00 A.M. to tutor Queen Christina of Sweden.) One story goes that while Descartes was in bed one morning, he thought of the x-y system as he watched a butterfly slowly flutter past a set of French doors—which have slats that form numerous crosses in the doors from top to bottom—in a kind of wave pattern. Descartes then probably said to himself, or even out loud, "Voilà!" (that's French for "There it is!") and numbers were put together with spatial relations like never before.

Gottfried Wilhelm von Leibniz (1646–1716)

High-school kids take algebra classes too, usually along with geometry, then trigonometry, then calculus. Other than being known as a famous rationalist philosopher in the wake of Descartes, Leibniz was a lawyer and, in many ways, we owe the modern form of codified law to his legal writings and work. However, Leibniz never intended for his philosophy of law to be turned into law codified in books.

Leibniz and Isaac Newton each independently invented calculus (for Rob, in high school it was more like cal-*clueless* because he totally sucks at math). This guy was a total genius who got his law degree in only one year and also invented the mechanical calculator and refined the binary system of numbers that acts as the basis for modern digital computation. One famous philosophical idea that derives from Leibniz is the *principle of the identity of indiscernibles*, which states that two things are identical to one another (not discernible from one another) if they have all of their properties in common. So, if Clark Kent and Superman share all of the same properties, then they're the same guy. The same goes for Diana Prince and Wonder Woman, as well as basically anything defined in a standard dictionary like vixen and female fox, as well as bachelor and unmarried male. Oh, and a great-tasting German butter biscuit is named after Leibniz—you gotta try the Choco Leibniz . . . Yum!

Charles-Louis de Secondat, Baron de La Brède et de Montesquieu . . . or Simply Montesquieu (1689–1755)

Montesquieu was a political philosopher and lawyer in Bordeaux, France, most famous for advocating the separation of governmental powers in his *De l'esprit des lois* (The Spirit of the Laws). Taking ideas from John Locke's *Second Treatise of Government* (1689) as a starting point, Montesquieu argues that the government of a society should be separated into executive, legislative, and judicial bodies, so that they "check" and "balance" one another in an attempt to curb potential violations of individual rights, favoritism, corruption, and most importantly, tyranny that invariably comes with the executive body (the king or queen) having too much power in a society.

"There is no crueler tyranny than that which is perpetuated under the shield of law and in the name of justice," claimed Montesquieu. Needless to say, this idea didn't go over well in eighteenth-century Europe where kings, queens, and popes thought they had a "divine right" to their despotic rule, and in 1751 the Catholic Church added *De l'esprit des lois* to its *Index Librorum Prohibitorum* (List of Prohibited Books).

Still, Montesquieu's work was widely read and became incredibly influential for all modern forms of constitutional monarchies and republics, including the UK and the USA. Thomas Jefferson, himself a lawyer, used *De l'esprit des lois* and *Second Treatise of Government* as blueprints for the US's Declaration of Independence and Constitution.

Jeremy Bentham (1748–1832)

Bentham changed the face of ethical decision making by offering one of the best defenses of *utilitarianism*, which is a theory stating that the morally correct decision is the one that maximizes the pleasure, benefits, or good consequences for all persons affected by it. Bentham's student, John Stuart Mill (1806–1873), further refined utilitarianism, and his name is most often associated with the theory.

One implication of utilitarianism is that the *end* of bringing about these good consequences can justify employing less-than-good *means* to achieve all of this good. Consider the hubbub about the US employing waterboarding and other forms of torture in the wake of the 9/11 terrorist attacks. People who think like utilitarians would say that the end of finding and stopping terrorists justifies the torturing of folks who know where these terrorists are located.

Bentham got a law degree in 1769, but never practiced. He proposed something called a panopticon (Greek for "all seeing"), a prison designed like a big cylinder with the inmates in cells all around the edge while guards were situated in a center hub with the ability to see them constantly, twenty-four-seven. The idea being that if you're always watched, you'll learn to act civilly—in Bentham's own words, it is a "mill for grinding rogues honest." If you want to read about—and see—something creepy, look up what was done with Bentham's body after he died.

H.L.A. Hart (1907–1992)

Hart followed many of Bentham's ideas concerning legal philosophy and, in 1961, published *The Concept of Law*, which is widely regarded as a seminal work in legal positivism. According to legal positivists, a legal system in some society is based on social rules and norms that are actually practiced.

Leslie Green writes that, according to legal positivists, law is "a matter of what has been posited (ordered, decided, practiced, tolerated, etc.)" As opposed to almost every legal philosopher since Plato who have argued that laws are grounded in some kind of natural or divine law, legal positivists maintain that laws are wholly social constructs.

Legal positivism can go hand-in-hand with *ethical relativism*, the thesis that what is morally right or wrong is wholly dependent upon your social circumstances and, hence, what's right in the USA can be wrong in some fundamentalist theocratic nation and vice versa. For example, in the USA it's morally wrong to deny a woman a fair trial if she shows up at the courthouse accusing a man of raping her, and also morally wrong for a mob to stone her to death out behind the courthouse for making the accusation. However, the same actions may be morally right in the fundamentalist theocratic nation and, according to the ethical relativist, this is all fine and dandy.

If laws are wholly social constructs too, as the legal positivists maintain, then apparently the fundamentalist theocratic nation can actually make it *legal* to deny the woman her right to a trial and stone her. Sounds strange, doesn't it?

Ronald Dworkin (1931–2013)

According to law as integrity, propositions of law are true if they figure in or follow from the principles of justice, fairness, and procedural due process that provide the best constructive interpretation of the community's legal practice." So maintained Ronald Dworkin in *Law's Empire* (1986), a seminal work in contemporary legal philosophy.

Anyone who studies American law, political philosophy, or legal philosophy is familiar with Dworkin's writings and his theory, law as integrity. Dworkin was one of Hart's students and actually offered a critique of Hart's legal positivism. If you read the previous paragraph, Dworkin would probably say that the principles of justice, fairness, and procedural due process can be applied cross-culturally to make it such that it's *illegal* to deny a woman her right to a trial and stone her. You need not appeal to nature or some god when recognizing that things like justice, fairness, and procedural due process should ground laws.

The Top Eleven Lawyer Jokes

11. Q: **What's the difference between a vacuum cleaner and a lawyer on a motorcycle?**

    A: *The vacuum cleaner has the dirt bag on the inside.*

10. Q: **How many lawyers does it take to screw in a light bulb?**

    A: *Three. One to climb the ladder, one to shake it, and one to sue the ladder company.*

 9. Q: **What do you throw to a drowning lawyer?**

    A: *His partners.*

 8. Q: **What's the difference between a good lawyer and a bad lawyer?**

    A: *A bad lawyer makes your case drag on for years. A good lawyer makes it last even longer.*

 7. Q: **Why does the Law Society prohibit sex between lawyers and their clients?**

    A: *To prevent clients from being billed twice for essentially the same service.*

 6. Q: **If you see a lawyer on a bicycle, why don't you swerve to hit him?**

    A: *It might be your bicycle.*

5. Q: **What's the difference between a lawyer and God?**
   A: *God doesn't think he's a lawyer.*

4. Q: **What's the difference between a lawyer and a liar?**
   A: *The pronunciation.*

3. and 2 Q: **What do you call a lawyer with an IQ of 100?**
   A: *Your Honor.*

   Q: **What do you call a lawyer with an IQ of 50?**
   A: *Senator.*

And the number 1. lawyer joke . . .

1. Q: **How many lawyer jokes are there?**
   A: *Only three. The rest are true stories.*

Equity Partners and Associates

KAREN ADKINS, PhD, is Associate Dean and Professor of Philosophy at Regis College in Denver, Colorado. She has published articles and book chapters in philosophy, mainly on gossip's contributions to knowledge. Her attempts at Wifely Goodness are regularly undermined by her cranky feminism.

JUDITH ANDRE, PhD, is Professor Emerita at Michigan State University. She writes on theoretical and practical ethics, to include medical ethics and business ethics. In retirement she seeks the good life, and *The Good Wife* has been part of that.

ROBERT ARP, PhD, is an analyst working for the US Army. He has authored or edited numerous books, book chapters, articles, and other works in philosophy and other areas. He agrees with Socrates that we should, "by all means, get married: if you find a good wife, you'll be happy; if not, you'll become a philosopher."

ANA CAROLINA AZEVEDO is a film school undergraduate at Unisinos (Brazil) and a former linguistics and translation student at the Federal University of Rio Grande do Sul (UFRGS) from Porto Alegre, Brazil. As an aspiring screenwriter, she watches TV shows like *The Good Wife* regularly, and she strives to be as good a professional as Alicia.

MARCO AZEVEDO, PhD, is physician and philosopher. His main field of study is moral philosophy, but he also has published articles and books in philosophy of law and bioethics. He was a member of the Regional Council of Medical Ethics of the Brazilian State of Rio Grande do Sul, which gave him good experience in professional ethics. He teaches in the Graduate Program in Philosophy at Unisinos (Brazil). He's an avid spectator of *The Good Wife*—thanks to his own good wife.

KIMBERLY BALTZER-JARAY, **PhD,** is a lecturer at the University of Guelph and King's University College (UWO). She is the president of the North American Society for Early Phenomenology, a writer for *Things & Ink Magazine*, and author of the blog *A Tattooed Philosopher's Blog: Discussion of the Type I Ink, Therefore I Am*. She once dreamt of being a lawyer like Jack McCoy but decided instead to become a philosopher because it seemed a more "just" career— no one dies or goes to prison when philosophers argue, and a lot less people want you dead.

ROD CARVETH, **PhD,** is Assistant Professor of Public Relations at Morgan State University in Baltimore, MD. In addition to over forty journal articles and book chapters, he's editor of *Mad Men and Philosophy*. Rod once toyed with the idea of becoming a lawyer, but decided to keep his soul instead. As Lenny Bruce once said, "In the Halls of Justice, the only justice is in the halls."

KATHLEEN POORMAN DOUGHERTY, **PhD,** is Associate Professor and Chair of the Philosophy Department at Notre Dame of Maryland University where she teaches courses in history of philosophy, ethics, and philosophy of education. She writes on character development, the construction of the moral self, and the role of personal relationships in the moral life. As a single mother with a full-time academic position, she's a fan of characters like Alicia Florrick, who give us all hope that we really can do it all . . . so long as we have a glass of red wine!

JOHN FITZPATRICK, **PhD,** is a lecturer in philosophy at the University of Tennessee, Chattanooga. He is the author of *John Stuart Mill's Political Philosophy: Balancing Freedom and the Collective Good* (2006) and *Starting with Mill* (2010). He's also a contributor to several popular philosophy books, which doesn't necessarily make him a virtuous individual, but does indicate that he practices the virtue of eccentricity.

JAI GALLIOTT is a philosopher working at Macquarie University in Sydney, Australia. He has published widely in the area of military ethics and has an interest in all things deadly. He *also* agrees with Socrates that one should, "by all means, get married: if you find a good wife, you'll be happy; if not, you'll become a philosopher." Only he adds that if you find a bad wife, you should retain a really good lawyer.

ROGER HUNT is a therapist and educator in Boston. He works to promote philosophy courses at the middle and high school level. He often reflects that perhaps having a good wife requires being a good husband . . . unfortunately.

SKYLER KING is studying English and philosophy at the University of Missouri-Kansas City. Besides writing for this volume and others, he's working on a novel that will (hopefully) be published upon completion. He thinks Alicia is ¡muy caliente!

JAMES EDWIN MAHON, PhD, is Professor of Philosophy at Washington and Lee University and Lecturer in Philosophy and the Law at W&L School of Law. He also teaches for the Program in Ethics, Politics, and Economics at Yale University. His primary interests are in moral philosophy, the history of philosophy, and the philosophy of law. But more than anything, he wants Diane Lockhart's corner office.

CÉLINE MORIN is a PhD student in Media Studies and a fixed-term lecturer in sociology at Sorbonne Nouvelle University. Her teaching and research interest focus on representations of women's loving relationships in fictional shows, meaning that her job is basically to write and talk about love all day. Even Kalinda is beginning to look like a Care Bear to her.

JENNIFER SWANSON is a graduate student and philosophy instructor at the University of Miami. She has published on ethical issues involving nonhuman animals, her main research interest and the subject of her dissertation. While she's never had the desire to be a lawyer, she must admit to the occasional urge to kick some ass in a pair of knee-high boots—faux leather, of course.

MARK D. WHITE, PhD, is Chair and Professor in the Department of Political Science, Economics, and Philosophy at the College of

Staten Island/CUNY, where he teaches classes in economics, philosophy, and law. He has also written and edited many books, journal articles, and book chapters in these areas. He did apply to Lockhart Gardner for the position of legal ethicist, but after humiliating Will on the basketball court he knew he had no chance of getting it.

Index